OUTWORK
THEM ALL

Wispy Willow Publishing
contact@wispywillowpublishing.com

ISBN: 979-8-9882000-0-0 (paperback)
ISBN: 979-8-9882000-1-7 (ebook)

Ordering Information:
Special discounts are available on quantity purchases by corporations, associations, and others. For details, visit www.seankling.com.

OUTWORK THEM ALL

A Gen X Guide to Business and Leadership Success

SEAN P. KLING

With utmost reverence, I dedicate this written endeavor to my beloved Katherine and Virginia, steadfast as a compass needle, guiding our shared odyssey through the vast oceans of imagination and adventure.

Contents

Introduction   1

1   Get Out of the Damn House!   7

2   How to Change the Atmosphere   21

3   Kitchen Cabinets Aren't Just for Kitchens   35

4   Rebound, Reinvent, Recoup   47

5   Running at Peak Efficiency   63

6   My Origin Story   77

7   Mistakes   89

8   Choose Your Heroes Wisely   101

9   Reading the Room   111

10   It Ain't Easy Being Green   119

Acknowledgments   129

Introduction

Building a business is hard, and knowing where to begin and how best to grow it can be challenging to say the least. Whether you're a small or midsized businessperson feeling stuck or someone just starting out, Generation Xers—or those of us born between 1965 and 1980[1]—have a recipe for your success.

Every businessperson wants to be successful, but not everyone knows the secret ingredients to reach that goal. Some of those valuable business practices and attitudes have been lost to younger generations. This book aims to present those practices, show you how they are rooted in my generation's upbringing, and discuss why they can work to help you achieve your personal and business aims.

Maybe you're just starting out or have frustratingly plateaued

---

[1] Amy McKenna, "Generation X," *Encyclopedia Britannica*, last updated January 2, 2023, https://www.britannica.com/topic/Generation-X.

and don't know where to go next. This book offers shortcuts to success that I learned the hard way—a mix of plain ol' on-the-job training and making a heck of a lot of mistakes along the way. Sure, that OJT roughed me up, but it really is the best teacher. And as the saying goes, knowledge is fun to have, but difficult to acquire. I agree!

In addition to providing insights I gleaned from my OJT, I want to share what has informed my success so that my hard times can help smooth your path to success. Our generation, like all others before and since, have been shaped—and rocked by—major economic and political events that dramatically shaped our opportunities and business outlook. Due to our lives as latchkey kids, we adapted to navigate that ever-changing, stony landscape.

This book is designed to help you skip over some of those difficulties that business owners inevitably face. It doesn't matter what business you're in, where you live, or how much money you make now. If you already have a formula for success, then great! But the issues I discuss in this book apply to those who want more business and less hassle. So, if you are an up-and-coming entrepreneur aiming to increase your bottom line *by at least 20% or more per year*, then read on to take advantage of the Gen X recipe for success.

If you've ever heard the term helicopter parents, you know they meddle in their kids' lives too much. Gen Xers had the opposite experience. Most of our parents worked, so we let ourselves in after school and entertained ourselves without supervision. We did our homework without prodding, and planned, bought, cooked, and served meals when the parents returned. We also did other chores like vacuuming and walking the dog. Not hard stuff, just not fun either. But we learned responsibility, self-reliance, flexibility, and time management. We even acquired the skill of budgeting money (and keeping track of our allowance). All these skills were indispensable as we stepped into the business world.

This background also explains why we are known for our fierce independence, which is a hallmark of any entrepreneur. We wanted to jump off the merry-go-round of status, money, and social climbing that permeates modern existence. We don't like having to live up to someone else's expectations or help them achieve their dreams. We also have our own ambitions, and it is these traits have helped us weather political, financial, and social storms.

There were tons of problems looming as we entered the workforce in the '80s and '90s, such as perpetual wars, the dotcom bust, 9/11, a steep decline in manufacturing jobs, and on and on. One of the biggest challenges stemmed from the birth of the Internet in 1983.[2] Gen Xers weren't digital natives like millennials and Generation Z kids are. But we quickly adapted and have used it to achieve a great advantage ever since.

These and other lessons have spawned a unique outlook and have helped many of us become leaders in just about every field: economics, technology, marketing, space travel—you name it. I want to share our Gen X formula for success as you start or continue your journey. You will leave with ideas you can draw upon

---

2   Caitlin McLean, "When Was the Internet Invented? What to Know About the Creators of It and More," *USA Today*, August 28, 2022, https://www. usatoday.com/story/tech/2022/08/28/when-was-internet-created-who-invented-it/10268999002/.

for years to come. Feel free to hand them down to your kids too.

Who I Am

First, a bit about my background and how I came to be a successful businessman and public insurance adjustor. I'm licensed to do business in 18 states, and I'm not about to stop now.

I grew up in a small town in Pennsylvania. My father and grandfather were both military men. My grandfather fought in WWII, while my father served in the Marines during the Vietnam War and was awarded a purple heart for his injury (he didn't let that stop him either). Their stories of hardships and challenges inspired me to join the Army after high school, hoping to earn their respect. Things didn't work out so well in the military and I was medically discharge after only a year. But I did learn about discipline.

As much as my parents and grandparents influenced me, the fact that I am a Generation X baby has shaped me in ways that differ from baby boomers (1946 to 1964), millennials (1981 to 1996), and Generation Z (1997 to 2012).[3]

I didn't come from a wealthy family either. My father bought a 1,000-square-foot house with help from the GI bill and a $5,000 loan from his grandfather. Believe it or not, though, that $5,000 came in the form of change he'd kept in a bowling bag he'd had

---

3   Michael Dimock, "Defining Generations: Where Millennials End and Generation Z Begins," Pew Research Center, January 17, 2019, https://www.pewresearch.org/fact-tank/2019/01/17/where-millennials-end-and-generation-z-begins/.

over the years! My parents drove a brown Chrysler Cordoba that looked like a big, brown boat. Fish sticks and boxed mac and cheese were dinner almost every night. My dad had only a ninth grade education. My uncle had a high school diploma. Yet, together, they built an incredibly successful business. I owe my work ethic to my parents, and I come from a long line of hustlers.

As for my education, I was definitely not a star pupil. In fact, I was even put in special education classes for a while. I was pretty good at football, so the teachers passed me through to the next level.

When I turned 30, I enrolled in DeSales University and studied military history. The rest of my education was in the school of hard knocks. And I do mean hard. I drifted from one job to another as a welder and pipe fitter, pharmaceutical employee, safety instructor, owner of a construction business, and bouncer in a bar. By luck, my hobby of studying military history led me to a job in the film industry. As checkered as this past may seem, I took away very important lessons from each position. Although I didn't know it at the time, nothing you do or learn goes to waste. It's all about knowing how to put those lessons to use in the workplace.

CHAPTER 1

Get Out of the Damn House!

We Generation Xers are squeezed in between the baby boomer and millennial generations. For those of us belonging to the "sandwich generation," we came of age just as computers and cell phones were taking off.

Most of us are adept at social media, texting, and all that good stuff. We have become savvy enough to work online just as efficiently as the younger generations do. However, we Gen Xers also know that while everyone is sitting around typing out message after message, just that one handshake will get you the job faster than you can say, "Hi, my name is…"

If you are a Gen Xer, you probably know about the power of personal interaction. Many up-and-coming entrepreneurs may need a reminder, though. So, if you spend a majority of your time on *Zoom*, *YouTube*, *Facebook*, and *LinkedIn*, this chapter is for *you*. The message is simple: ditch the computer, get out of the house, and meet people in person. Just this one piece of advice will make all the difference in your bottom line.

This invaluable lesson in life was taught to me by my father. It's important to learn about people on a personal level. Interact with clients. Take them to lunch. Go to a baseball game. Create a bond that has nothing to do with business. See what they're like over time. This helps them to trust you, and in turn, you get to know about them. What makes them tick? What are their interests?

While this might seem logical for some, the problem is many of us spend a lot of time on the internet. I mean, *really* a lot! Some of this is because the pandemic kept us trapped in our house for too long. We felt lucky to have the internet and our phones to continue doing business.

A *Zoom* call may make it *seem* as if we are interacting, but we aren't really. It's fake interacting. At best, it's a poor substitute for taking the measure of the person. Of course, we see faces and hear voices. And sure, their expression, especially their eyes, tells us a lot. But are we *really* communicating with that person? For me, shaking someone's hand tells me volumes. Firm? Fishy? Do they meet my eyes? Grab my forearm? And that's only the beginning. I get none of that on *Zoom*. In person, I can observe so much more about their body language. Do they fidget? Do their eyes dart around? Do they check their phone every whipstitch?

Whether this person is honest or reliable may not be quantifiable with a measuring tape, whether online or in person, but our gut sure knows what's going on and is constantly registering reams of data. That's why we have the expression, "I get the impression that… That gut of yours is always on alert when it comes to sizing up a potential client or service provider. Does she interrupt? Turn toward you when you speak? Cross his arms when you're talking? So much of our communication is nonverbal and involves body language, and yet, how much body language do we see on a *Zoom* call? Only a fraction. In the end, you are making decisions on very thin data.

What's worse, during a PowerPoint presentation or webinar, we might not even see the speaker's face at all. Or we are told to mute ourselves! I don't like being muzzled like a dog. I've even seen audience members turn off their video camera. So, muted audience members can't speak, and the presenter can't see them. And *that* is considered communication? I think not.

The technology we often use today does not lend itself to smooth exchanges. Turn-taking, for instance, is awkward on a video call. When I'm in my potential client's office, I can see or sense if he wants to say something. These clues help me adjust to the listener's needs. But on *Zoom*, I feel lost.

Then there's the awkward way we stare at the other person (whether listening or speaking). This is so unnatural! In person we never do that because it's too intimidating—hostile even—to hold someone's gaze that long. I won't even go into what it would mean to date someone on *Zoom*. Yuck! Do you think you could make a reliable decision about who that person is just by seeing them on a flat screen?

Okay, so *Zoom* has its flaws and is better than nothing. Consider, then, how alienating it is when we post to social platforms. Now we don't see *anyone!* Somehow, we have an imaginary, ideal receiver for our information. How weird is that? And, while we're at it, how do we measure success on social media? By how many "likes" we get? *Big whoop.* Can we even call that communication? Plus, where are you when you're posting to those sites? That's right. You're inside in front of a computer or your phone, and that means you are *not* meeting people.

Don't get me wrong. I do my share of communicating online. But I don't stay at home waiting for the phone to ring—or worse, keep posting all day on *Facebook* or *Instagram*, eagerly awaiting my likes to pile up. In the end, those "likes" are merely an empty number whose initial rush quickly fades. It's a mirage. While you might think you're communicating, you're not. That said, some companies do depend on the internet to drive business to their site or store. Unfortunately, those likes might not even help you build your business or generate repeat customers. So, what am I left with? Imaginary readers who "like" you. You don't know their names or have a clue about their personality. How satisfying is that?

Then we have the heavenly *YouTube* channel that consists of nonstop, one-way videos. There's no question that it's useful. I consult it when I need to repair a chair or have an issue with my printer. But I'm not fooled into thinking that the person yammering on about this or that service or product has an inkling who I am. Do this, don't do that, they drone on. At the very least, it's an inefficient way of going about sales. Statistics show that over 500 hours of video are uploaded *every minute* worldwide.[4] Holy Time Waster, Batman! Too many people pushing too many goods and services. How are you to choose? Or conversely, how are you to get their business? I'll tell you how: You need to get out of the house.

Three wildly successful Gen Xers who learned this lesson and who have inspired me: Elon Musk, who was born 1971, founded SpaceX, Tesla, Inc., The Boring Company, Neuralink, and OpenAI, and is worth billions;[5] Jeff Bezos, born in 1964, founded Amazon and Blue Origin, and like Musk, is among the richest men in the world;[6] and finally, the owner of Rockstar Energy Beverages, Russ Weiner, was born in 1970 and has also done very well for himself.[7] What is it, do you think, that all these men had in common? Did they sit around all day posting photos of their yummy-looking veal piccata or goofy friends wolfing down Jell-O shots on social media? No. I mean, *hell* no! They dreamed big and then acted.

Let's look at how Russ Weiner made his fortune. He's a classic example of someone who built his company by taking his product to the people. Son of famed radio talk-show host Michael Savage, Weiner showed quite an entrepreneurial spirit even as a kid. He

---

4   L. Ceci, "Hours of Video Uploaded to YouTube Every Minute as of February 2020," Statista, January 9, 2023, https://www.statista.com/statistics/259477/hours-of-video-uploaded-to-youtube-every-minute/.

5   Erik Gregersen, "Elon Musk," *Encyclopedia Britannica*, last updated February 16, 2023, https://www.britannica.com/biography/Elon-Musk.

6   "Jeff Bezos," *Encyclopedia Britannica*, last updated January 8, 2023, https://www.britannica.com/biography/Jeff-Bezos.

7   Robert Frank, "The 50-year-old Founder of Rockstar Just Got a $3 Billion Check from PepsiCo," *Forbes*, accessed February 15, 2023, https://www.forbes.com/profile/russ-weiner/?sh=622842667268.

owned a yard service company at the age of eight, then worked at Wendy's in high school.[8] After graduating from college, he sold spring-break trips to Hawaii and Mexico to students. Although he lost his bid for a seat in the California State Assembly, he caught the eye of the owner of Skyy Vodka, who gave him a job. Soon thereafter, Weiner pitched an idea to his boss to have Skyy Vodka create a new energy drink. His boss wasn't interested. "Too many on the market now," was his reply. He did have some seed money from his parents, but kudos that he parlayed it into a lot of dough.[9]

But Russ wasn't deterred and moved forward with his energy drink plan at time when social media was in its infancy.

Here's how he rolled out his product. First, he bought an old limousine and had Rockstar's logo painted on the side. He hired several eye-poppingly gorgeous models to ride along in the limo to promote the drink. He drove around San Francisco visiting store owners and stopping by large festivals, all the while giving away free cans of his new product.[10]

When Russ introduced himself, he would say something like, *I'm living the rockstar life! I have a limo and these lovely, young women on my arm. Do you want to be like me?* Ka-ching! How many *YouTube* videos do you think it would have taken him to equal that

---

8   Ibid.
9   Taylor Nicole Rogers, "Rockstar Energy's Extravagant Billionaire Founder Russ Weiner Just Sold His Company to PepsiCo for Nearly $4 Billion. Here's How the Son of a Far-right Talk Show Host Built a Multibillion-dollar Energy Drink Empire," March 14, 2020, https://www.businessinsider.com/meet-rockstar-energy-drink-billionaire-russ-weiner-pepsi-sale-2020-3.
10 Ibid.

kind of success? Uh, maybe none? He could have sat there all-day long fiddling with email lists and posting messages on *LinkedIn*. Instead, he took a chance and laughed all the way to the bank in his limo because never gave up.

The success did not end there. In 2020, PepsiCo offered Weiner $3.85 billion for his company. His energy drink ranks as the third most popular brand today—all because he got out of the house.[11]

Musk also began his entrepreneurial career early. He decided against attending Stanford to start his own web software company in 1995 with his brother and a friend. He fired up SpaceX when he was only 31 years old.[12]

Elon has a nerdy presence about him. He's had 10 kids with I don't know how many women.[13] But none of that matters. People admire and respect him. He accomplished that by pressing the flesh and doing what he does best: promoting himself in person. Do you think he'd have gotten any sponsors to fund his SpaceX company if he'd peppered potential investors with requests on email? "You don't know me, but could I please borrow $1 trillion to start my new company?" Hardly.

---

11 Kristin Stoller "Rockstar Energy Drink Founder Cashing Out for Nearly $4 Billion, Says the American Dream Is 'Alive and Well," March 11, 2020, https://www.forbes.com/sites/kristinstoller/2020/03/11/rockstar-energy-drink-founder-cashing-out-for-nearly-4-billion-says-the-american-dream-is-alive-and-well/?sh=65686f5375d.

12 Raisa Bruner,). "AComplete Timeline of Elon Musk's Business Endeavors," *Time*, April 27, 2022, https://time.com/6170834/elon-musk-business-timeline-twitter/.

13 Brittany Miller, "Who are Elon Musk's Kids? His 10 Children's Names, Ages and Mothers," July 19, 2022, https://pagesix.com/article/elon-musk-children/.

Jeff Bezos has a similar story. He graduated from Princeton in 1986 with a degree in electrical engineering and computer science. He founded Amazon in 1994 at the age of 30.

Amazon began as an online bookstore that has since mushroomed into the marketing behemoth it is today. He has been so successful that he has been dubbed the first centibillionaire and is worth over $150 billion. He's also in direct competition with Musk's SpaceX company, founding his own aerospace manufacturer and sub-orbital spaceflight services company, Blue Origin.[14]

Here's the point. When you're sitting at a computer, information comes at you at breakneck speed. Everyone is telling you that you've got to buy their free product to prevent baldness, get six-pack abs, and make your first million. And there you are, chewing on beef jerky, popping M&Ms, and consuming their hype. It's the recipe for going nowhere fast.

The key is this: Nothing is free, and if these hucksters say you don't have to pay to get it, then *you* are the product.

Show *Genuine* Interest in People

I mentioned above that my father said to interact with clients and get to know who they are as a person. Hunt, kill, eat, he'd say, meaning you find what you want and go get it. I researched what I wanted to be and what I wanted to be like. Then, I listened—

---

14 "Jeff Bezos," *Encyclopedia Britannica*, January 8, 2023, https://www. britannica.com/biography/Jeff-Bezos.

hard—to the people I was with.

One day, this guy Joe Spillone and I were having coffee. I mentioned that I always wanted to be in films. He said he'd introduce me to the director of a film he was working on so I could try out for a part in the movie. What did I have to lose? I was all in.

As it happened, the company was making a film about the Mexican American War. Well, I thought to myself, I'm a history buff and know a huge amount about that war and have even given lectures about the Mexican War. Joe told the director about my background, mentioning that I knew just about all there was to know about this era, including how people dressed. So, when I looked at the actors on the set and saw they were wearing clothes that were not historically correct, I told the director.

Soldiers at that time wore baggy uniforms and duck-bill hats—not the tight-fitting costumes the men were gussied up in for this film. Since I'd served in the Army, I also had knowledge about period weaponry and insignias but did my best not to come off as a know-it-all (easy does it when you correct someone). The director asked if I could help with costumes. I was so eager at the offer that I about jumped out of my skin. I worked for a whole month every day. Okay, it was for free, but I enjoyed it and felt flattered that they were willing to take my advice.

After that gig ended, I started getting calls from people who had worked on that film saying, "Hey, we're doing a film about police in the 1940s. Could you come help us?" Next thing I know, I'm sitting with Bruce Willis and James McAvoy on the movie set of *Glass* talking about aspects of the film and what would look historically correct for that time period. I also appeared in an episode of *Law & Order* as a police officer.

When these opportunities came about, I made sure I spun them all into gold. Sure, I could have taken lots of selfies with these famous people and had a lot of fun. Instead, I asked them about themselves. I wanted to connect with them on a personal level. I talked to stars like Ice-T about growing up. I asked him about how he got into movies and started his successful music career. These were all people who had achieved success, and I wanted to know how they'd accomplished it.

Everyone else was starstruck and busied themselves by taking selfies. I wanted to be their equal. When you're taking pictures and putting celebrities on a pedestal, you're already at a disadvantage because you're not relating to them as people. When you take the time to get into their head, you learn to read them—even if they're an arrogant a-hole. And if you do discover they're too self-involved and arrogant to be helpful, then you know not to work with them. You've saved yourself time and effort.

I wouldn't be where I am now in my public insurance adjusting business if I did not meet people and interact with them on a personal level face to face. Just as you need to trust others, prospective clients need to trust you, feel secure, and know you are genuinely interested in them. When you can accomplish this, they don't think you see them merely as a wallet you want to pickpocket. This personal touch has earned me lots of clients in the past.

One day, I got a call from a contractor who helped clients with storm damage to their roofs. He wanted more information about my services. "Can you meet me at IHOP?" he asked. We chatted about his business over coffee. I found him affable and had no problem relating to him. Then, out of the blue, he said he didn't have a license to assist people with insurance claims in Florida (where I live) and asked for my help. The upshot is that I ended up having lots of policies to work on. He even paid for the coffee.

You can flatter someone over the phone or write glowing emails about how you'd like to work with them in the future. Instead, take someone to a rock concert, get tickets to a hockey game, or just give them knickknacks like key chains and fountain pens with your logo on it. This kind of personal touch can be priceless.

Listening to people is one of the most precious skills you can cultivate. When you listen, you can learn a lot. When you talk, you don't. But your interest must be genuine. People can spot a phony from miles away. Nothing says sincerity like being attentive.

I do have one caveat about listening, though. Take notice if the effort you put into a relationship is more than you gain. Feel them out, talk to them, and find out about them. Remember something about them that sets them apart from others and write it down if you must. Build on that social interaction. People thrive on that.

And for God's sake, remember their name. In 1936,[15] Dale Carnegie, in his still-popular book, *How to Win Friends and Influence People*, wrote, "A person's name is the sweetest and most important

---

15 Jessica Weisberg, "What Dale Carnegie's 'How to Win Friends and Influence People' Can Teach the Modern Worker," *The New Yorker*, April 2, 2018, https://www.newyorker.com/books/page-turner/what-dale-carnegies-how-to-win-friends-and-influence-people-can-teach-the-modern-worker.

sound to that person."[16] It says you are important to them.

Humans are pack animals. We travel in groups. You take that away from people and they stumble. We don't do well in isolation, as has become all too obvious from the pandemic the world has suffered through. Remember this: Good social interaction means good business.

Steps You Can Take

If you're shy, here are some tips to help you get up and out. Ask yourself, *What am I interested in?* Accounting, sports cars, dogs? Then, research who you'd like to meet (in person!). Find out who's in your area or who you might have a connection to through a friend or organization you both belong to. Are you interested in banking? Maybe talk to the loan officer at your local branch. Ask if they have advice for what your next steps might be to get into the field. Think of it as educating yourself.

Here is a trick I pulled to introduce myself to potential clients.

One day, I went to Payless Shoes and bought 20 pairs—women's and men's—that didn't fit me. Then, I took one shoe out of each box and mailed the packages to several people I wanted to talk to. "Now that I have one foot in the door," I said in the enclosed note, "I'd like to come and tell you about myself and my business." You'd be surprised how many people wouldn't try a simple technique like

---

16 Dale Carnegie, *How to Win Friends and Influence People* (New York: Pocket Books, 1998), 85.

this to meet people. You don't even have to be that creative. Just pick up the phone and ask if you can meet. The worst they can say is no.

Informational interviews are popular nowadays. To go about setting up one of these interviews, here's what you'll need to do:

1. Determine the career field you'd like more information about.

2. Find a person at that company to interview. You can do this by contacting Human Resources of the company or organization and ask who might be the best fit for your inquiry.

3. Develop a brief introduction about yourself and why you're interested in meeting.

4. Contact the person by phone, email, or *LinkedIn*.

5. Make an appointment to visit him or her and don't forget to confirm it. Ask if it would be more convenient to talk by phone.

6. Prepare for the interview. Gather several open-ended questions you genuinely want answers to. Have them at the ready because they may agree to talk right off the bat.

7. Let them know your background and your interest in them or the company. Emphasize you are *not* looking for a job (even though you might be).

You will be surprised how welcoming people are. If you doubt that, just imagine someone calling you to find out more about you and your route to success. Yes, flattery works on *everyone*. It must be genuine, though. Nothing stinks to high heaven more than an insincere compliment.

—— Takeaways

→ Get off your duff and meet people in person. Communicating online can help, but it will only take you so far.

→ Remember people's names.

→ Ask about what matters to them. Take an interest in their families, spouses, work, and hobbies.

→ Read their body language to find out who they are.

→ Find common topics to discuss to build rapport around.

→ Don't ask for favors. It always puts you in jeopardy because, if they don't pay you back, it's the end of the friendship. They may never offer anything either, but that's okay. A friend is a friend is a friend. We all need more of them in our lives. Besides, you never know how that relationship will pan out, either in business or your personal life.

And that's the point. You *never* know.

CHAPTER 2

How to Change the Atmosphere

When did we all get so sensitive? I ask myself that almost every day. People can't say anything anymore without having someone jump down their throat for whatever reason. That's what this chapter is about—how you can cool things down and choose employees who don't have those tendencies. I call it changing the atmosphere—the tone, the mood, the vibe—whatever you want to name it.

No, it's not easy to do, but it will sure make life better for you and for those around you—whether you have a company of 10, 100, or in the thousands. Doing so will definitely affect your bottom line positively too.

That atmosphere, or your company's culture, is composed of several elements. Among them are your employees, hiring and firing practices, and, most importantly, you. You'll need to see a breakdown of those elements to see how it works, and I'll pitch in my advice at the end to guide your transformation.

As with everything in this book, my theories are based on Generation X values. We Gen Xers are known to be fiercely independent. After all, we were left alone a lot to fend for ourselves. We map that trait onto our workplace habits and philosophy. But being independent doesn't mean we are not able to get along with others. On the contrary, we have been quite successful in the business world. With that being said, we do have our limits. One example is that we don't put up with much guff from employees or colleagues. Let me explain.

The Problem

We want the work atmosphere to be stress free, fun, and the big one—*not* politically correct. Year after year, I find that people who push their values in your face create the impression they're being victimized. This attitude causes other employees to walk on eggshells because those "special" people have an agenda that we don't—or can't—know about. At the end of the day, everyone is different. We all come from a background that has shaped our thinking and emotions. But how am I to know what your triggers are?

Let me give you an example of a time I offended someone without knowing it.

One day I went to pick up some papers at an attorney's office. I had referred many insurance claims cases to him over the years. As I walked into the office, the receptionist came out. She was young, probably under 30 years old.

"Can I help you?" she asked.

I told her why I had come. "My name is Sean. What's yours?"

"My name is Stormy."

"Oh," I replied. "As in Stormy Daniels?"

She gave me a weak smile and said, "Yeah, I guess."

I got the papers and left.

The attorney called me later that day. "Hey, Sean. I gotta ask you a question. Did you refer to Stormy Daniels and Donald Trump when you met my secretary? You can't do that. It made her feel uncomfortable."

Now, I didn't want to jeopardize the excellent working relationship I had with this attorney, but I thought, *uncomfortable*? For likening her to a person in the news she didn't like? How was I supposed to know that?

I saw red.

"I just have to tell you," I said after taking a few moments to gather my wits. "I understand that you gotta do what you gotta do. But you are calling me on the carpet because I merely referred to someone who had slept with Trump?" I let the comment hang for a bit, then said, "I will no longer be referring clients to you."

This is a perfect example of what I mean by atmosphere. That young woman was hostile, and for a reason I thought held no merit. Now if I had said something like, "Oh, are you a porn star too?" then the attorney may have had a point. But I didn't come anywhere near saying something like that.

Now, whoever goes into that office has to watch what they say. Here's my question: Do you want to have someone in your company that is so politically correct, so offended by the most minuscule thing on *Facebook* or anywhere else—especially as a receptionist? Our one exchange that lasted probably 30 seconds has now hurt his business. That kind of attitude sours the ambience for everyone in that office. Now they have to tiptoe around and examine every word that comes out of their mouth. Or worse, avoid her at all costs. It makes for a tough working climate, hurts production, and can result in a joyless place to work. (I will say that though I had these harsh feelings at the time, I came to view the exchange differently as the years passed.)

What happened to relaxed, free-flowing conversation? What happened to the kind of office where telling jokes around the water cooler was accepted, like in the popular movie *Office Space*?[17] The film satirizes the everyday work life of a typical mid-to-late-1990s software company. At the heart of the film are a few individuals fed up with their jobs. But they joke about it. They don't bash people

---

17 *Office Space*, directed by Mike Judge (1999; Los Angeles, CA: 20th Century Fox, 1999), VHS.

over the head for a remark that some thin-skinned colleague happens to find offensive.

I ask you, when did we become so sensitive?

When you're in that kind of an atmosphere at work, employees focus on what you say rather than on the work at hand. I strive for an atmosphere with less stress and more fun. Remember, it's not just a business. It's a place where people spend a large part of their day with people they did not choose to be around. So, everyone needs to bring tolerance and understanding when they walk through the door.

Obviously, the best idea is not to hire those folks in the first place (more on that later), but once they're in your employ, they become a cancer.

Causes

I lay the blame for a lot of this squarely at the feet of social media and the news channels. While I believe people are inherently good, they can't help but be influenced by an avalanche of biased stories. One month we see people waving a Ukrainian flag, then the next month brandishing placards with fetuses. News consumers become brainwashed by the current way of thinking. It's wherever the political wind is blowing. How do you get away from that?

I'll tell you what Gen Xers are doing. We're exiting certain kinds of social media big time. We want to get away from the shock media. We don't want to wallow in that kind of biased, angry, fear mongering that occurs day after day. It sets off people's flight or fight response. Take me, for instance. If I listen to those channels on the way to work, all that gamma radiation from the negative news turns me into the Incredible Hulk—ready to smash everything in my path. I have to swallow a bunch of chill pills before talking to anyone. So, I stay away from it.

I especially dislike people who claim they're a victim. With them, it's always, "Oh, my parents were mean to me," or "that person has a nicer car than mine," and the "I would have made more money if I'd gone to college" kind of stuff that I do my best to avoid.

Solutions

We need to step aside from political correctness, general negativity, and those who whine about being a victim. Doing so doesn't take away people's rights. We need to sit back and laugh at ourselves. This will allow us to change the atmosphere. All you have to do is look at the funny side of the many ridiculous things that happen to us every day.

Then we need to look in the mirror and ask, "Am I creating these problems that we're dealing with? Am I attracting the wrong kind of people into my company? If so, how?"

As a first step, I advise relaxing the atmosphere of victimization. Here's an example of someone who had nothing to do with victimization.

Cornell Turner was an old Black man when I met him. I loved Cornell. He was one of the finest men on the earth. He also didn't feel victimized. He didn't feel that his skin color was the reason for his victimization. My grandfather grew up at the same time. The two of them used to laugh about the good ol' days. I remember one time when we were working in my dad's office, the power went out. When my dad and I made our way to the back of the shop, we heard someone rustling. Oh no, we thought. Someone had broken in.

"Who's back here?" my dad asked.

"It's me."

"Whose me?" my dad said.

"It's Cornell."

"Smile so I can see you!" my dad joked. They laughed and laughed. Cornell had gotten stuck back in the shop without a flashlight. Neither one of them looked at it as a racial thing.

Cornell said no one ever called him an Uncle Tom because he was friends with White people. As a matter of fact, at my grandfather's funeral, when we put him in the grave everyone drifted off except Cornell. He was the last person to leave. You'd think that two guys who grew up in the most segregated part of the world would never be on the same page.

My grandfather also invited members of the Rosebud Sioux tribe to his house. They weren't offended in the least by the TV shows that showed cowboys and Indians fighting. In fact, they joked about it. In my opinion, humor is the way to go. Forget all this victimization stuff. It's no fun, and no one benefits.

I carried this light-hearted attitude over into my own life. My dear friend Mark is half Japanese and half White. His father had been in a Japanese internment camp in WWII. Despite his father's bad treatment by our government, Mark loved the U.S. more than anything. He had no bad feelings over it. In fact, we used to rib him about his Japanese heritage. We'd say, "Hey Mark, my Japanese DVR is broken. Can you fix it?" You could say those things back then. Not now. You'd be crucified every which way on every social media platform there is.

It's one thing to *say* people should relax and stay away from people who are so politically correct they choke the life out of any interaction or plead victimization to the point of absurdity, but it's quite another to deal with an employee with that attitude. Of course, there will always be aggrieved people. But, like Stormy the receptionist who got bent out of shape because I supposedly called her a porn star, people need to chill. It's good for their blood pressure, makes for a more accepting world, and is just plain fun.

You might well ask how to do that. After all, it's not easy to spot these kinds of buzzkill people who pollute the atmosphere with these personality traits. Here is my recipe for interviewing employees for my insurance consulting business. I think you'll see that your business will thrive if you consider these points.

I assume you know what questions are illegal in any job interview: age, citizenship, disability, gender, marital status, race or ethnicity, and religion (look out for several in the gray area too). But if you follow these guidelines, you won't offend anyone, and you will be on your way to finding those who share your values.

First, listen to your gut. This may seem like a nebulous piece of advice. But you can practice becoming conscious of a very faint tickle in your stomach that says, "Hmm, something's off about this person. I can't identify it, but I just don't have a good feeling." That isn't a reason to deny them a position right off the bat. But it is worth listening to it. Give it time, and the answer will become clear.

Look at their shoes, hair, and clothes. If I own a construction business, I might not care if someone comes in with dirty shoes, a tattooed face, or a nose ring. In the insurance business, though, people expect a person who is more down the middle. So, if that individual comes in wearing, say, a shabby outfit, I think that person doesn't invest in himself. Conversely, if he's wearing an expensive suit and tie, it may be too flashy for insurance work. Either way, my antennae go up. In my occupation, people like to do business with someone who wears more moderate attire.

My grandfather could tell who someone was just from their hands, eyes, and shoes. I always check those out when I meet people too. Shoes tell you where you've been. If they're in construction, they may have muddy boots. So, that's not a surprise. But if they wear those same muddy boots to my interview, then it's a red flag. What kind of car does the person drive? Read their body language and watch their eyes.

Listen to what they say. Some people are skilled liars (see my chapter on mistakes I've made a little later on). Believe me, I know all too well what it's like to get bamboozled. But you can't know everything—especially if you're just starting out. Besides, those liars have been perfecting their schtick for many years, so they fool unsuspecting people like you and me all the time. As seasoned as

I am as a businessman, I've been taken too and I'm a sadder but wiser man because of it.

Look at how they walk. Is their head bowed? This could be a sign of depression. Do they walk with purpose and confidence? This might be a good sign. As mentioned in the previous chapter, people signal who they are in all kinds of ways. Do they meet your eyes when you are introduced? Do they seem self-assured?

I hope we've all gone beyond judging people by their ethnicity or color because it's definitely *not* the right yardstick. Plus, it's illegal. But if I'm sitting across from someone wearing a T-shirt sporting a slogan from a known radical group who has blue hair and blood-shot eyes and then goes off on a rant like bad-mouthing a previous boss, they probably don't blend in with my company's culture. They might be a perfectly fine person, but I need to consider my other employees and the kind of person they will feel comfortable working with.

My company is small—eight employees now—so I don't have a Human Resources Department. This is partly by design, since I feel that once I give power to another person to hire and fire, then my values may not be respected, and therefore will not be reflected in the people they hire for me. Of course, I could ask to interview them, too, as a final stage before they come on board. But it seems a useless and unnecessary step—not to mention costly. So, I do all the hiring and firing. Maybe that makes me a control freak, but remember, we Gen Xers are known for our independence, resourcefulness, and self-sufficiency.

Growing up, we had to handle a lot of situations on our own, so it makes sense that at this point in my career, I want most things to be within my control. It's why I work for myself. I've been quite successful with that approach. If you own a large company (or plan to), you probably don't have the time to do the hiring—especially if there are lots of departments requiring variously skilled people.

All I'm saying is that you need to be careful about who you hire. So, if you have a chance to interview them at any point in that process, be aware of their body language, their appearance, and their language.

Another way to weed out people who are potentially incompatible with your company or your values is to ask them questions that help to inform you of what kind of person they are. I do this by asking scenario-based questions.

Here's an example of a hypothetical values question I might ask. "What would you do if you saw some employees stealing toilet paper from the company? Would you A) help them steal it; B) report them to the supervisor; or C) not say anything at all? That might be an obvious question to answer correctly, but you get the idea.

You could also ask several indirect or open-ended questions that would begin with "What would you do if... " It could be a job-related question, perhaps something that you devised from an experience you had with another employee who did you wrong. Someone's values are not hard to discern when you ask these type of questions.

I believe in meeting prospective employees multiple times. The goal is to get a read on their behavior in different kinds of circumstances.

What is their writing like? Ask them to write a business letter to an imaginary client who has been complaining about your company's service. How do they handle it? They may not have a position that requires writing letters to clients, but they certainly will be writing emails—even if it's just internally. One unfortunate email or letter can put you out of business in a heartbeat.

—— Takeaways

1. If you make a mistake by hiring someone who doesn't work out, it may not have been something you could have avoided. A solid analysis of where you went wrong can sharpen your interview techniques next time so you won't repeat that mistake. Forget the idea that you can ever be perfect at this process. However, over time you will slowly begin to sense which people you feel could harm your business.

2. Instead, move forward with a group of people who will help you reach your business goals.

3. Stay away from the idea that everything needs to be politically correct. It stifles others and puts a damper on interactions.

4. Be alert to people who claim to be a victim.

—— Action Steps

1. Look over who you have already employed. Who has been a successful employee? Why are they successful? Have they exceeded your expectations? How did that person perform in the interview? Did you have any doubts about them at the time?

2. By the same token, analyze where you may have gone wrong in hiring employees who didn't work out. Ask yourself how you can tailor that process to eliminate those pitfalls in your interviewing process.

3. Think about terminating employees who are a cancer on your business. Why are they not working out? Look at ways of terminating or replacing them, or try absorbing their work into other avenues. Look into putting out job postings (with discretion) and look at resumes that align with your goals and values in mind.

4. Have them write a letter to a client who has complained about your product or service. They will be writing emails, and you need to see if they can express themselves coherently and with reasonably good grammar and tone.

5. Hire slow, fire fast.

—— Must Dos

1. Check their credentials. This can include:
   - Diplomas

     - Licenses or certificates

     - Career experience they claim on the resume

- Their overall moral compass (It's challenging to gauge that but it's important. Do this by asking open-ended questions like the toilet paper scenario or think of a scenario that is pertinent to your business.)

2. Meet with the potential employee several times in various venues (lunch or dinner, in the office) and introduce them to other employees to get their impressions (if this seems appropriate). The time in between meetings gives me time to think about what questions I'd like to ask next time and pay attention to any warning signals that crop up (that's the gut check I mentioned above).

3. I don't hold much store in job recommendations. Anyone can put down anything for a reference. There is always the hidden trap of reading a glowing recommendation from a previous employer who wanted to get rid of an annoying employee.

4. If you do check on recommendations, I suggest talking to at least one of them—say a supervisor at their company. Even then, ask that supervisor who else that person might recommend you talk to—someone *not* on the candidate's list, like a co-worker, secretary, or manager of another department they have done work for. You will be more likely to get an honest report.

In the end, it pays to surround yourself with like-minded people who have similar values, whether it's a similar work ethic, attitude toward work, willingness to pitch in when needed, personality, and, it goes without saying, competence at their job.

CHAPTER 3

Kitchen Cabinets Aren't Just for Kitchens

Many Gen Xers tend to be cynical about trusting authority.

With our parents so busy when we were kids, we often had to fend for ourselves. We also grew up at a time of eroding confidence in the government and the economy—and an energy crisis and other problems taught us how to be more resourceful and reliant. We learned not to just take things at face value, but to seek external guidance—a trend that's continued into adulthood.

Andrew Jackson had Gen X energy. When he became president in 1828, the bruising campaign made him distrust the official Washington so much that he got together an informal circle of advisers. He was mocked for openly for this, and his opponents jokingly called it his "kitchen cabinet."[18] Jackson stumbled on a terrific idea, especially for us Gen Xers who tend to be cynical about trusting authority. If you have a little of that cynicism with your own kitchen cabinet, you're never going to make hasty, rash decisions.

I consider my own kitchen cabinet the cornerstone of my business. My advisers provide expertise I will never have, keep me motivated, and help me through tough times that would have otherwise done me in. For this reason, keeping a group of close advisers around you can have great merit.

Just as the most successful sports teams are not a set of individuals, companies are not just you. You can't be omniscient, and like me, you probably have some strengths but not all that are needed to be successful. The trick is to find others who have the ones you lack. With that said, it's not easy to find these trusted counselors. This chapter outlines why it's important to build your team, who and how you should choose its members, and what benefits you will glean.

A board of directors is valuable for many reasons, but they do not serve the same purpose as this kind of inner circle. A company's board are often selected for their fundraising prowess to fill company coffers. Nonprofits also have boards, but they have no monetary investment in the enterprise. They do it for political reasons,

---

18 Robert McNamara, "Kitchen Cabinet—Origin of the Political Term," ThoughtCo, last updated February 22, 2019, https://www.thoughtco.com/kitchen-cabinet-1773329.

to stroke their ego, or to be in control. Of course, it would be a mistake to paint all of them with a broad brush. In my experience, these kinds of board members tend to be tyrannical. Moreover, the selection process can be a popularity contest. We Gen Xers are typically not out to impress others—we try to impress ourselves.

None of that works for me. My advisers seek a common goal—to keep my company flourishing. They don't make any profit from my sales, although they are paid well. Just as I can't own a sailboat by myself, I may go in on it with some friends to pool our money and expertise. Together, we can soon be setting sail for Treasure Island. I would have run the boat aground in the first five minutes if I'd tried it myself.

Here are some reasons to have a solid team in place:

1. You have trouble seeing into the future.

2. You're bad at paperwork.

3. You're clueless about marketing.

4. You failed algebra and have trouble balancing a checkbook.

5. You don't like hiring or firing people.

There are more reasons, but you get the idea. Analyze your strengths and weaknesses, then begin thinking about who can fill those chinks in your armor.

Who to Invite

Who will serve you best depends on your business. I like to keep my circle to no more than five. This low number means we are a sleek, nimble group devoid of the bureaucracy found in bigger businesses.

These are my must-have advisers: a financial expert, business developer, operations manager, marketing team member, and a "blood brother." Other slots you might fill are a researcher/visionary, team coordinator, life coach, and people-person to do outreach. These might seem superfluous if you have an employee that does one of these functions already. But the purpose of this body is to advise you with the expertise and experience of an outsider.

You can find a marketing, financial, production person more easily than you can the central figure in this circle: your "blood brother" (or wing man). By that I mean a person who you're in sync with either through shared experiences or even by blood itself, like a sibling, spouse, or life partner. This position should be filled by someone who has nothing to gain and has your best interests at heart. Most people spend their entire lives looking but and never find one. It could be a spouse or a partner. Whoever it is, it should be someone you have known in various challenging circumstances and would trust with your life.

Look for a person who dug that foxhole with you or stood by your side through messy times. There's a reason you see war veterans embrace each other after many years apart. It's a bond forged in the heat of disruption, chaos, or loss. Look for a person who wants to fight that fight with you.

Anybody can write anything on a resume. You have to decipher through the BS. People put a big picture out there to impress people, but finding a good team member takes research and time. You're not just going to start looking and then tomorrow immediately find one. This process can involve a lot of trial and error. You have to kiss a lot of frogs to get a prince, and the person who's the most boisterous is liable to be the worst team member.

I'm reminded of the kinds of veterans who have served in the military and have seen combat. They don't talk about what they did in the Marines or Army. It's those who weren't in the military who embellish their stories. I'm always leery of people who are the most boisterous. I stay away from them.

It's a mistake to hire on emotion and not on need. Take the time to strategically define those candidates. The real gems might not be on listed on a job board or social media. Anybody's who's worth anything will probably have to be stolen from someone else. Be patient. It takes years to build a team, and it will constantly change along with your needs and, of course, their performance. Don't hang on to people who do not fit the bill.

Where to Look

You must be constantly on the lookout for people of this caliber. You may make a mistake and enlist someone who fills the void at that time. But life changes and so do businesses and their needs. You may find that you depend on some members of your circle more than others and may be in constant contact with them during various times, like the financial person during tax season or the marketing person during a rollout of a new product. Some are fulltime while others are contract workers for short-term projects (for instance, if you need someone write a business plan). I don't have formal meetings with my group. Some business owners may *Zoom* with them each day. It depends on how many members are in the group, the problem at hand, or the amount of strategizing required for a project.

This brings me to the question of how many people you should have in your inner circle. The answer will depend on the size of your business. I'm in favor of odd numbers. A group of highly professional and knowledgeable people will always have discrepancies. As my dad used to say, KISS (keep it simple, stupid). The more people you have, the more complications or personality clashes can arise.

Of course, there will be personality conflicts. They occur when any group of strong-willed and intelligent people gather. With fewer people, say, three, alliances between two members may form, allowing that pair to gang up on the other one. If you have five, there is usually one person who is neutral.

While all the positions are crucial in their own way, the marketing person has a special role. If you don't have money coming in, then the business will sink like a stone regardless of how competent the other cabinet members are. You can muddle along doing finance and operations by yourself for a time, but marketing requires someone with the fire in the belly to get things moving, and quickly.

Then consider the operational aspects. This is where Gen X values come in. They are different from those of baby boomers. They put the factory together and produced the widget. But when it came to operations, we rolled up our sleeves and did it ourselves (or subcontracted it out). We knew that unless we did that, it would mean standing on the dock and waving goodbye to the goods as they're shipped off to Mexico, India, or elsewhere.

Finance is next. We're the last generation that could buy a house that wasn't crazy priced. We had a mortgage. We used to pick out toys from the Sears catalog and eagerly wait for the package to arrive several weeks later. Now, we pay for something online and get it the same day. We used to be able to buy a pickup truck for $10K. Now a Ford F-150, the most popular pickup, starts at $35,000. We've watched the greatest rise in prices of goods of any generation. This kind of inflation makes one quite cautious about investments and expenses. So, the finance person should be savvy about financial trends and keep an eye on the finance department to guide them in making decisions about where to bank, where to get the best credit, how to structure a company should we invest in the stock market, and so forth.

You could include a life coach on your team, too. This is someone who doesn't even need to know about your company or interact with the others on your team. As time goes by, even the best group can get tunnel visioned. An outsider such as a life coach can come in with fresh eyes and ideas because they're not embroiled in the politics that inevitably arise even with a relatively small group.

Reach out to executives, retired people from your industry, and those who run similar businesses. Their track record is easy enough to verify. I've heard of some business owners who have poached good advisers from other companies. Doing that depends on how many enemies you want to make in your field. In general, though, people who work as unofficial advisers do so because they enjoy taking risks and are not usually employed full time. Some people have a certain level of risk. Some of them must have a level of risk.

Excluding Company Employees

I exclude employees from my inner circle for a couple of reasons. First, they have an employee mindset. Most are there for a paycheck and aren't focused on the bigger picture. I want leaders on my team. Employees are not visionaries or leaders or they would have started their own company. It's hard to make that transition from employee to leader because they're not independent thinkers. It's like the three different levels of kids in high school. There are the kids going to college, another group that attends vocational education classes, and those who are in general education. In my high school, the vocational ed kids wanted to learn a skill that was valuable, like plumbing and roofing. College prep kids wanted to go on to bigger and better things and aspired to become things like an accountant or attorney. General education people were destined to become employees. We need all three groups of people in our society. In my company, I need people with both vision and critical thinking skills.

Gathering Data

These kitchen cabinet members also provide a valuable service by getting feedback from employees, vendors, and clients. Sometimes, I'll hire a polling agency to monitor the temperature among employees. Other times, an adviser will casually strike up a conversation with a vendor over coffee, or with an employee when they're working without alerting them to the fact that the discussion is evaluative.

Employees should be monitored often. Besides letting them air their grievances, it's good to have them let off steam by whining and complaining. In an old military adage, good soldiers complain, but if they stop complaining then you know they don't care anymore. All that is valuable information. You don't have to let it turn into a bitch session, but there's always some truth in why they whine. All this feedback is *especially important* and informs how you run your business.

When I put out my feelers, it also tells me some important details about employees' behavior and can expose themselves for what they are. We had to let one guy go because he was getting greedy and was not pulling his weight. He was allowing everyone to do the work for him and not bringing in sales, which was part of his job.

You must pull that cow away from the teat and send them on their way. Otherwise, he's holding you hostage in a way because he or she is occupying the place of someone who could be more productive. To ignore that kind of employee means you've given up then reins.

Sometimes I give out a questionnaire. However, I generally find these to be unreliable since only the angry employees fill them out. Regardless, it's another way to gather data, and it does give them the opportunity to voice their opinion. To check on employees' production during the day, I look at my CRMs (customer resource management that are my guidelines for how to interact with customer) and check sales. I log into our phone portals and check their messages to see if employees are returning clients' calls. Some people would call that micromanaging—I call it protecting my investment. We do monthly or quarterly surveys.

I also pay attention to the body language for unhappy workers. If I start to notice that they make a lot of mistakes, are fighting with their coworkers, and come in late and leave early, I consider those to be red flags. People speak with their actions more than their words.

In the end, we use this information gleaned by my inner circle to hone our policies and direction. And, as with the gentlemen mentioned above, we may also use it to decide if we should fire someone. Those are hard decisions, but we must make them. You wouldn't keep an old, worn-out pair of shoes even though they're comfortable. We're in business to make money, not friends. Friends don't pay bills.

—— Summary

Surrounding yourself with highly competent, nonemployee advisers is a must. With all the moving parts to running a business, your kitchen cabinet can focus on different aspects you might miss— your personal blind spots. My recommendation is to hire advisers who are experts in finance, business development, marketing, and production management. A fifth person could be an outsider like a business consultant or coach. One of these people is your wingman (or woman) who is intimate with your vision and will fight alongside you to achieve that goal no matter what. Generation Xers may be cynical about authority because of our experiences with election fraud, junk bonds, big government, forever wars, etc. But that experience has hardened us.

—— Takeaway

You can't be all things to your company. So, bringing several trusted advisers into your inner circle will help guide your ship. It takes a long time to develop a solid core group of advisers, but it's an indispensable move that will help your company over the long haul. Not all advisers are needed permanently. Some may not be as useful as your company grows, and some may be hired to fill a temporary need, such as writing a business plan.

—— Steps

1. Determine what kind of advisers you need for your company.

2. Consult retired business owners and others in your field to get leads on dependable candidates for these positions.

3. Look for people who want to fight that fight with you.

4. Review their usefulness and productivity to your company often.

5. Keep the number of advisers low. This minimizes the risk of becoming too bureaucratic.

6. Choose an odd number of advisers. This keeps the group from becoming deadlocked.

7.   Use these advisers to gather feedback about what employees, vendors, and clients think about your products and services.

CHAPTER 4

Rebound, Reinvent, Recoup

Gen Xers know all about rebounding.

We've faced so many economic, political, and institutional setbacks. All those challenges presented obstacles we had to be creative to overcome.

It helped that we grew up on the greatness and legacy of heavyweight boxer Muhammad Ali, who lost five matches in his 21-year career—including his infamous fight against Joe Frazier.[19]"The Greatest" made darn sure he didn't lose to "Smoking Joe" a second time. How? He worked out harder, changed some techniques, and studied his opponent's moves.[20] That's the same recipe I recommend for any up-and-coming entrepreneur.

We use a lot of metaphors from the world of boxing when talking about business. We "duke it out" for customers, "take the gloves off" when dealing with competitors, and "throw in the towel" when we lose everything in the stock market.

I would be lying if I said you won't get hit below the belt at least once. And that's just the first year. I've been gut punched several times. But the thing is, you *cannot* surrender. Just as Ali did after he lost against Frazier, you must get up, spit out the broken teeth, and come out swinging.

This chapter is about rebounding from whatever knocked you down. It doesn't matter how stunned you are. What counts is getting back in the ring. Below are some notable examples of those who have met the challenge, along with some tips for you to avoid getting sucker punched in the kisser in the first place.

First, you'll want to avoid crying in your beer about your failure. Ali didn't lie on the ground whining about getting walloped by Frazier. It made him angry, so angry that he then went on to

19 Luke Beirne, "The 5 Men Who Beat Muhammad Ali," last updated May 12, 2022, https://www.sportskeeda.com/pro-boxing/the-5-men-beat-muhammad-ali.
20 Allan Binoy, "When Muhammad Ali Avenged His Loss to Joe Frazier," Sportskeeda, last updated January 29, 2022, https://www.sportskeeda.com/pro-boxing/news-muhammad-ali-avenges-loss.

avenge that loss by winning his next two matches against him.

No matter your business, making a comeback presents the same challenge in all fields. One Gen Xer who stands out and is a good example of this is Robert Downey, Jr. Born on the cusp of the Gen X cut off in 1965, he was a talented actor and producer who had great success in his youth. He won an Academy Award for his portrayal of the title character in the biopic *Chaplin*. Unfortunately, he fell prey to substance abuse and legal troubles and went into rehab.[21] He joined the cast of *Ally McBeal* but was fired from that show because of more drug charges.[22]

This revolving door at the rehab center, along with his legal troubles, led to difficulty getting a completion bond to insure he would fulfill his contract. His track record was horrible and the insurance company had good reason to deny him the coverage. Insurance companies never bet on a weak horse.

Downey could have stayed on that downward spiral of drugs and jail and ended up like his pals who OD'd. But he has reportedly been sober since 2003. It's called reinventing yourself. It takes Herculean strength to overcome that kind of an addiction. Hats off to him.[23]

---

21 John Cunningham, "Robert Downey, Jr.," *Encyclopedia* Britannica, last updated August 12, 2022, https://www.britannica.com/biography/Robert-Downey-Jr.

22 "Downey Fired from Ally," ABC News, April 25, 2001, https://abcnews.go.com/Entertainment/story?id=106083&page=1.

23 John Cunningham, "Robert Downey, Jr.," *Encyclopedia* Britannica, last updated August 12, 2022, https://www.britannica.com/biography/Robert-Downey-Jr.

As a counterexample, take Robert De Niro (born in 1943, so not a Gen Xer), who made his name with films like *Taxi Driver* (1976), *Deerhunter* (1978*), and Raging Bull* (1980),[24] and who doesn't know when to quit. The result has been a string of awful movies in his later years.[25] He has not been selective and has just taken whatever roles come his way. He's not able to let go. Chill out, De Niro, you're ruining your legacy by maintaining the same persona you had decades ago. De Niro has reportedly been taking on roles due to financial issues. But he should have bowed out of acting in my opinion, or at least been more selective of his roles.

Just as De Niro has become a watered-down version of himself, your company may also be hanging on to its glory days too long. When this happens, it's time to reinvent. Stay ahead of the pack and don't lead from behind. Your company may be heading for the graveyard unless you stay on top of what's ahead in your field.

Now, take my all-time hero, Ethan Suplee. He totally rejiggered his image to get out of a huge rut in his film career. In the 1990s, he was cast as the chunky bully in the popular TV series, *Boy Meets World*. He was always typecast as the fat kid, but, as he aged, he was offered fewer and fewer roles as a grossly obese adult. He thought his acting career was over. He found solace in alcohol and yet more food. At his heaviest, he weighed in at 525 pounds. His health began to decline and with it fears he'd never see 50. It was a

---

24 "Robert De Niro," IMDB, accessed February 13, 2023, https://www.imdb.com/name/nm0000134/.

25 Anne Helen Petersen, "The Shaming of Robert De Niro," Buzzfeed News, January 20, 2016, https://www.buzzfeednews.com/article/annehelenpetersen/the-shaming-of-robert-de-niro.

do-or-die moment. [26]

Then, he turned his life around. Big time. He was determined to get six-pack abs by the following year. He started walking around the block every day, riding his bike, and watching what he ate. By 2011, he had peeled off about 300 pounds, and got his desired washboard abs. He started getting some cool roles in hits such as *The Wolf of Wall Street* (2013) (which was nominated for a Best Ensemble Cast award), the TV show *Twin Peaks* (2017), and the series *Good Girls* (2020).[27]

All this happened because he didn't stay stuck.

The sports world offers some other dramatic examples—some good, some bad. Peyton Manning is a terrific example of someone who shucked his football image after 18 seasons in the National Football League as the star quarterback. Peyton was recognized as one of those rare athletes alongside Joe Montana, Wayne Gretzky, Michael Jordan, and Tiger Woods,[28] who, it is said, have a way of looking at a playing field that others don't. They're like chess masters who see patterns that we mortals don't recognize.

Peyton knew when it was time to hang up his cleats and leave the

---

26 Rachel Paula Abrahamson, ""How Actor Ethan Suplee Has Maintained His Nearly 300-pound Weight Loss," *USA Today*, January 21, 2021, https://www.today.com/health/ethan-suplee-weight-loss-actor-went-550-255-pounds-t206343.

27 "Ethan Suplee," IMDB, accessed February 15, 2023, https://www.imdb.com/name/nm0839486/.

28 "The Greatest Athletes of All Time," Sunny101.5, May 31, 2017, https://mysunny1015.com/2017/05/31/the-greatest-athletes-of-all-time/.

field. He was 40 when he won his last Super Bowl ring.[29] He said in a press conference that he was going to have a beer and retire. The Golden Boy of the NFL could have written his own ticket as a coach, TV commentator, or even an owner, but he said no. He then got involved in Papa John's pizza franchising. But when its owner got into hot water, he had the good sense to terminate his ties.[30]

Peyton, and his equally famous NFL QB younger brother, Eli, lend their names to charitable causes like hurricane relief work,[31] a golf classic for the blind,[32] and kids on the autism spectrum.[33] He is the king of reinvention.

Tom Brady, another uber-famous football star, has not wanted to let go until recently. The media often razz him about his age.[34] He's been beset with injuries and must work out twice as long as

---

29 "Peyton Manning's Super Bowl Wins," Sportskeeda, last updated February 6, 2023, https://www.sportskeeda.com/nfl/peyton-manning-super-bowl-wins.

30 Mary Vinnedge, "Peyton Manning and Papa John's Franchise: The Full Story," FranchiseWire, June 1, 2021, https://www.franchisewire.com/peyton-manning-and-papa-johns-franchise-the-full-story/.

31 Marsha Walton, "Manning Brothers Team Up for Katrina Relief," September 5, 2005, https://www.cnn.com/2005/US/09/04/mannings.relief/index.html.

32 John Fennelly, "Eli Manning Will Host Guiding Eyes for the Blind's 45th Annual Golf Classic," June 11, 2022, https://giantswire.usatoday.com/2022/06/11/new-york-giants-eli-manning-will-host-guiding-eyes-blind-45th-annual-golf-classic/.

33 Cody Adams, "Peyton Manning Children's Hospital Nurses Take Part in Special Training," WishTV, November 11, 2022, https://www.wishtv.com/news/local-news/peyton-manning-childrens-hospital-nurses-take-part-in-special-training/.

34 Louisa Thomas, "Tom Brady Got Old," The New Yorker, February 1, 2023, https://www.newyorker.com/sports/sporting-scene/tom-brady-got-old.

the younger team members to keep up. Tom, I'd tell him, you gotta leave the game because it doesn't love you anymore. Fame on the field has not protected him from personal problems with his marriage to Gisele and their divorce.

Rebounding happens to ordinary people who struggle with setbacks all the time. One of those folks (not a Gen Xer) is a dear friend I knew all my life until he died at age 62. Steve Kitchen worked for my father as a millwright (aka. industrial mechanic). He was a whiz at installing and repairing systems like conveyors, packaging equipment in mass production facilities for foods, plastic, or lumber. These were humongous projects and involving complicated machinery.

Steve wasn't just a tradesman—he was an artist. He mentored me to do the same by teaching me how to work with my hands and make things I could be proud of at the end of the day. He could look five steps ahead, like a chess master, to anticipate—and avoid—what might go wrong.

Steve's skills outstripped those of anyone else in the field. Now consider this: he was handicapped. As a young teen, he was involved in an accident that led to the loss of vision in one eye. Instead of pitying himself or taking handouts, he learned the trade of millwright from his father.

He realized early on that many career choices like truck driver or the military were not available to him. So, he chose a job where he could succeed, and he became the best he could be at his job. In short, he's a stand-out example of someone who reinvented himself. His ability to adapt to his handicap speaks volumes about him—especially since he had to make that a decision at such a tender age.

Steve Jobs, co-founder of Apple and pioneer in the personal computer industry in 1976, is another example of a (non Gen X) man who reinvented himself after being forced out of his own company nine years after he started it in 1985. Okay, he said, I'll take my marbles and set up NeXT, a computer platform development company. He eventually hooked up with Pixar animation studios to contribute to popular animated films like *Toy Story*.[35]

That isn't the end of Jobs' transformation. Within a few years of Jobs' departure, Apple's stock plummeted. They were facing bankruptcy. Board members realized that Jobs had something special they couldn't duplicate. So, they swallowed their pride and begged him to return. He consented because Apple was his baby. But the important Gen X and Y thing Jobs did was to turn his sights elsewhere once he faced an earthquake in his life and get on with what he loved most. Sadly, he died too young in 2011 at age 56 of pancreatic cancer. But he gave us a prime example of how to reinvent in the face of obstacles.[36] Apple remains one of the world's leading companies today.

All these examples have shown what these people have done after meeting with a change in fortune. True, actors can keep acting until they die, and athletes have a timer on their bodies that runs

---

35 "Pixar and NeXT," About Steve Jobs, accessed February 13, 2023, https://aboutstevejobs73.weebly.com/pixar-and-next.html.
36 John Markoff, "Apple's Visionary Redefined Digital Age," *The New York Times*, October 5, 2011, https://www.nytimes.com/2011/10/06/business/steve-jobs-of-apple-dies-at-56.html.

out at a certain age. But they all inevitably faced the what-do-I-do-now question.

So, what would *you* do after your company or career ends? And have you thought about what you should do now to avoid that outcome in the first place?

Here are some suggestions.

Let's start with your company and its perils. First, you may think, *hey, my company isn't dying.* That's the mantra of many failed companies, or those that have at least scaled back their enterprises. Take, for instance, Circuit City, Toys "R" Us, Yahoo, *Myspace*, American Apparel, AOL-Time Warner, and the way other huge, successful companies may have felt until they hit tough times. The issues that contributed to their problems were myriad—among them poor decision making, not retooling for new trends, not monitoring their competitors' products, poor leadership, and so on.

Now let's talk about what you should do *before* your business fails. My advice—and this is my point to all business owners—set up a protocol for monitoring the danger signs. Plan contingencies for those times when your business begins to show the first signs of wear and tear so you can apply the brakes. Not doing so means you'll go down into the drink like the musicians on the Titanic.

Look into the future. Stay awake. No one has a crystal ball but there are signs. Pay attention to declining sales and employee turnover because the press will seize your misfortunes and begin ridiculing you mercilessly. Once that happens, there will surely be a decrease in revenue to buy supplies. That leads to empty shelves, which in turn means having to cut employee hours. Cue the funeral dirge.

Read. This step alone will help you recharge your mind and outlook. I know doctors who devote a whole day during the week to read the latest news about drugs, procedures, and so forth. Why should you be any different? I bet you expect your physician to be up-to-the-minute with information. Without doing that, doctors stand to lose patients, and you may lose your livelihood. Reading history books is especially enlightening. See how other cultures and peoples solved their problems.

Speaking of history, there's an interesting tale about what happened to the great Greek city-state of Sparta in terms of reinvention. Every time Greece was invaded, the Spartans would defend their sister state, even though the Spartans and Athenians were enemies. But the Spartans didn't diversify their male population. Instead, they stayed married to the warrior code. As the Roman empire grew, the Romans, who used to vacation in Sparta, soon began looking at its inhabitants like people regard the Amish today—as a quaint relic of the past.[37]

There's no Greek state of Sparta anymore. The Spartans were great when the world was violent, but they never educated their population to become engineers, philosophers, or doctors. Everything was focused on the warrior mindset. Sparta eventually became a caricature of itself and ended up a tourist attraction.

---

37 Simon Hornblower, "Ancient Greek Civilization," *Encyclopedia Britannica*, November 28, 2022, https://www.britannica.com/place/ancient-Greece.

Conduct market research. Put feelers out to clients about what they need and want. Solicit polling and give out questionnaires, as I mentioned in the previous chapter. Study the results. Stay abreast of new trends and technology in your field. Research the next generation of buyers.

Weed out employees who have gotten stale or disinterested in their jobs, hence the call for "new blood" for fresh ideas. It's not that old blood is necessarily bad. Longtime employees have institutional memory and perhaps company loyalty, too. Those are valuable traits that you don't want to discard out of hand. Weigh all that against the prospect of your company going belly up.

Is there a way to reinvigorate employees? I am asked this a lot. I am dubious because, even if you give them vacations or promotions, something at work triggered that dissatisfaction. How much more time do you think you will get out of them? A month? A year? They've already mentally checked out and will be biding their time until they can bolt. This isn't the 1930s when people spent 30 years at a job. Now people stay three or four years max at any one job because Gen Xers came to realize that companies weren't loyal to us.

Diversify. Just because a product or service works now doesn't mean that path won't swerve into a ditch. Don't depend on just one client for all your business. If you do, they can pull the carpet out. If you have a janitorial business with a contract to, say, clean the offices at a university, think about expanding your client list to include hospitals, for instance. It may mean enlarging your workforce, but if one of these customers cuts fires you, you have a safety net. Then you can move on without too much of a hiccup.

The bank Wells Fargo is a good example of a business that branched out. It started as a mail-delivery service via stagecoach (still the company logo) in 1852. But if it had stayed delivering goods with ponies, it would not have become one of the biggest banks in the U.S. today.[38] Think of what happened to the two of the biggest names in communication: AT&T and Western Union. Nobody's communicating with them anymore.

AT&T made a basic business error by sticking to its narrow idea that voice communication would continue happening over its circuits. It didn't see that communication was between people and that they would seek out other less expensive ways to accommodate that need, such as cloud-based video conferencing.

Rapidly changing technology also eventually put The Western Union Telegraph Company out of business. Founded in 1851, it dominated the communications industry until the 1980s when it became a money-transfer company. It was eventually absorbed by other companies after experiencing financial problems.[39]

Two giants that bit the dust.

Listen to speakers like authors and tech experts. I thoroughly enjoy listening to retired military officers and great historians like Steven Ambrose. These speakers have spent their whole life learning a specific trade. They have something to say.

38 "History of Wells Fargo," Wells Fargo, accessed February 13, 2023, https://www.wellsfargo.com/about/corporate/history.

39 "Western Union Financial Services, Inc.," Encyclopedia.com, 2018, June 11, 2018.
https://www.encyclopedia.com/social-sciences-and-law/economics-business-and-labor/businesses-and-occupations/western-union-telegraph-company.

Travel. Go places like an art museum or science center. And please don't forget our national parks, like Yellowstone, that have so much natural beauty than it's almost impossible to behold all of it. It can give you a completely different perspective on life and business when you realize how big the world is, how powerful the ocean is, and how quiet the forest is. Not all education comes in books. Family vacations are a super way to educate your kids. No need to splurge by going to Switzerland. The U.S. is vast enough to entertain even the most jaded traveler.

Meditate. We live in a world with a lot of noise. Meditation allows your thoughts go in and out. It also gives you time to regroup. It's like a spa treatment for the brain.

Other advice. If you see the danger signs that your company is failing, it might be too late. But if that is the case, I suggest not cutting jobs; reinvent them instead. If I'm in X business and it's starting to become antiquated, you might well ask, how do I catch up? For the love of God, don't make excuses like we didn't spend enough money or lost our shirt in the stock market. Instead of blaming something or someone, look at *doing things* to reverse the trend. Blaming doesn't get you anywhere.

—— Summary

Business owners can't sit on their laurels even if they're having a banner year. Things can change on a dime, like markets, vendors, technology, and consumer needs. The ground is constantly shifting. So, it behooves everyone to be look out for the next trend, write an updated business plan, and create a few blue-sky ideas just for the fun of it. Otherwise, you'll eventually become like the cemetery caretaker—there will be plenty of people under you, but nobody will be listening.

The problems we face today are not unique. They may be unique to our era but not to history. All that we're experiencing today has happened before and will happen again, and war, famine, infections, and tyrants are among them. Centenarians born during the 1920s can give you a 360-tour or how their world has changed. They went from horse and buggy to watching drones fight our wars. Now that's a world view.

—— Advice

Stay away from the garbage on the internet. Articles drawing you in with click bait that leads to hype and junk—not to mention all those twerking videos. It's nothing but content created by people who are crying for attention with the sole purpose to sucker you into buying information or a product. Find more reliable sources.

Keep abreast of market research and put feelers out to clients about what they're looking for. Solicit polling and give out questionnaires. Study the results for clues to changes that are afoot. Stay alert to new trends and technology in your field. Research the next generation of buyers.

Attend lectures and listen to books on tape while you drive to work.

Read, read, read, read, and read more. Books, magazines, and (especially) newspapers are great options to improve your knowledge and overall intellect.

Meditate. Let go of your thoughts. They will come back to you dressed in entirely different clothes if you let them.

Take a family vacation. These trips don't have to cost a lot or be weeks long. Go to a museum, an amusement park, petting zoo, or nearby lake—things that will keep kids away from their computer and phone.

—— Steps

1. Stay alert to the warning signs of a company in trouble.

    - Are your sales slumping? Market share decreasing?

    - Are you laying off employees?

    - Are you starting to get bad press about the health of your company?

2. Monitor your employees' opinions and productivity. Are they satisfactory?

3. Stay abreast of market trends.

4. Schedule time to read.

5. Attend lectures.

6. Cut back on the internet surfing. There are very few ideas there. Besides, if you do find one there, that means that five gazillion other people saw the same thing.

7. Meet with industry leaders. Take them out to lunch. Ask their opinion.

8. Diversify. Don't stay with just one client or customer. You're asking for it if you do.

CHAPTER 5

Running at Peak Efficiency

When Gen Xers started out in business, we used a Rolodex, slow-as-a-tortoise word processors, snail mail, so-so photocopying machines that broke down a lot and didn't collate or staple, and, yes, some of us sniffed ink to get high. The whole operation was grossly inefficient.

In time, businesses became cloud-based. Now we use Google Drive for photo and document sharing. That one product got rid of a mound of hassle with lightning-fast scanning, copying, pasting, faxing, and editing—not to mention reducing spam emails and postal costs. So, I'm not damning all software. Just the kind whose supposed benefits don't really improve your bottom line.

There's no shortage of products hawked to business owners about how to run their business more efficiently. Many goods and services touted to end your business woes come with big promises and even bigger price tags.

As business management guru Peter Drucker said, "Efficiency attempts to do things right...Effectiveness is concerned with doing the right things."[40] Well said, Peter, but you forgot to add how difficult that is to achieve.

This chapter attempts to fill in some of the details that Drucker hints at in his quote, such as how to be more efficient. Specifically, forgoing costly software that can bog down output, hiring practices that can hurt your business, and an overly fussy protocol for procedures.

Software

Every day, I see ads for customer service management (CSM) software peppering social media sites and cluttering my email inbox. Improve your business by 50%! Run your company at peak efficiency! Now the bad news. This will happen if *only* you shell out big bucks for that miracle. Beware, because these products have hidden costs, and paradoxically, can *decrease* efficiency. In time, paying their exorbitant fees could blow a hole in your budget

---

40 Peter Drucker. "Do you do things right, or do the right things?" March 6, 1965, The Financial Post, Newspapers.com.

and make you lose time due to a steep learning curve and buggy software.

Let me save you some of that time and money by explaining how to be choosy about what services, software, or gizmos to buy. Before you click that buy button, think about all the hassle it will be to train employees on a new software program or incorporate a new tool into their production line. Then, figure in the downtime it takes to train and implement it. Recently, I went to a grocery store to return a product I couldn't use. But when the cashier went to complete the transaction, she fumbled around, muttering something about the new software they'd just installed, and finally had to bring in a manager. Meanwhile, I was frustrated and so were the patrons waiting impatiently behind me. What should have taken 30 seconds lasted almost 15 minutes.

So, newfangled software that promises the moon can affect customer service as well as play havoc with your books. In another time-eating fiasco, I eagerly unpacked my brand new printer, naively thinking I could merely turn it on and print. Hardly. It took me a whole afternoon to get the darn thing running. I had to log on to the company site, download their instruction manual, and when it still didn't work, I waited online for an agent to untangle the mess. It turned out that it didn't work on my 5G Wi-Fi, and I had to create a 2.4G pathway for it. It turned out to be four hours flushed down the toilet. The lesson I learned from this is that it's a pipedream to think you can just plug and play with new devices and software.

New software rarely works right off the bat. It often has bugs that you weren't warned about when interfacing with your existing system. Then you have to get a patch for it and hope it will finally work. I know you have your own stories. Bigger companies have IT staff who can handle this. But smaller businesses may not have the luxury of creating a position to handle these kind of issues for you. These are the kinds of companies that are most vulnerable.

Let's take another example of a service I think is a waste of time: search engine optimization (SEO). It's designed to improve the appearance and positioning of web pages in organic search results. "Work with expert SEO professionals," they hype, "and increase your website's traffic and conversions."

Most of it is a hoax, and an expensive one at that. A quick check of pricing revealed that a one-time project may typically run between $5,000 to $40,000. Hourly rates for SEO consultants range from $150 to $1,200 per hour. So, while that company is raking in your cash, you may not see any results for around six months. By the way, how do you measure its efficacy? The only people who're getting rich are these SEO blokes. There's that flushing sound again.

So, paying for it doesn't always have the outcome you might expect. In many cases, you're better off hiring a subcontractor (although see below about that), or even better, an in-house employee to do the work. That way, you don't have to explain something to someone who doesn't know anything about your business. Plus, you can monitor the people, progress, and process. External companies who offer this software are not invested in your culture and systems. Most of the time, an employee is.

Hiring

Another what-looks-like-a-good-idea is 1099 hires, aka temporary gig workers. As a Gen Xer, when I started working everyone got a paycheck. Certain guys did the welding, others operated a crane, and so forth. Then companies got the bright idea to hire people who work for themselves to circumvent paying payroll taxes and benefits. These people are either a project or specialty hire. Problem is, they don't work for you. They have no vested interest in your company, its welfare, or its efficiency. When the job is done, they go on to the next assignment, and so on. Of course, it's financially more appealing. But all that glitters is not gold. When employees are on your payroll, they have loyalty to your brand because they don't want to lose their job. Contractors don't share that same goal. Also, and maybe I'm paranoid about hiring outside contractors, but how do you know they're not divulging secrets to another company?

Then there are the temp agencies that place employees for up to 90 days. After that, they usually allow the company to hire them permanently. The problem I've found is that these temps work up a storm for those 90 days, and then 30 days after they're hired they're not so interested. I call those people Rent-a-Drunks. Temp agencies are seductive for the same reason 1099 hires are—because it means getting out of payroll taxes. Stay away from them and instead find people who are interested in your business and want to help it grow.

So, before you plunk down $39 a month (or $468 for a year) for some magic system that claims it will help you streamline, save money and time, increase productivity, organize, or otherwise improve your bottom line, think about setting up your own policies and procedures. Determine your target demographic and ways to reach them, hire quality customer service representatives, collect client feedback, and simplify the systems you have now. It's all hard work, of course, but it pays off. Chasing rainbows does not.

Procedures

Let's go back to defining what efficiency is for *your* company. Does it mean producing more widgets per hour, increasing the number of pools your servicepeople can clean in a day, or boosting the amount of drywall workers can hang in a week? Only you can define that. But I do have some advice for making this decision.

Perhaps you've decided to increase efficiency by retooling your protocol for processes, practices, and procedures. I'm all in favor of reviewing those aspects of a business. But if you find you're adding steps to that protocol, don't! As you know, a cornerstone of my business philosophy is to simplify. So, for goodness' sake, don't create *more* steps for people to follow in your zeal to be more productive. Adding too many can become expensive, confusing, and tedious—real zeal-busters. If employees get mired in too many policies and procedures, it stifles progress—not to mention overcomplicating things that puts a drag on efficiency.

Making it simple was exactly why the Operation Warp Speed program worked so well. The goal was to accelerate the development, manufacture, and distribution of vaccines for the

COVID-19 virus as soon as humanly possible.[41] It was a huge and unprecedented undertaking. Developing a vaccine usually takes several years to create, but because of the super-high mortality rate, officials approved the vaccine in six months! Why? Because they removed the usual policies and procedures. Things got done pronto. They did away with the red tape along with the myriad steps and regulations.

The pandemic, although still a threat, was largely mitigated. Vaccines continue to play a vital role in decreasing the number of cases through the many shots and boosters that have been delivered to arms around the world.

So far, I've discussed choosing software and employees wisely and decreasing the steps in your protocols. That's good advice for those with existing businesses. But what about aspiring entrepreneurs? What should they do to launch their business?

First, I need to point out that not everyone is a good businessperson. Look at yourself and ask, "What do I know about marketing, manufacturing, and quality control? Do I know how to hire the right people and how many?"

Then, decide on a plan of attack. Most people are good at a skill they've learned from a job or education. That may be a big part of the reason you want to start a business in the first place. Are you a software engineer and want to develop an app for other engineers? It may seem easy to do because you know the field and

41 "What Is Operation Warp Speed?" National Institute of Allergy and Infectious Diseases, July 1, 2020, https://www.niaid.nih.gov/grants-contracts/what-operation-warp-speed.

your audience so well, but that's just a baby step toward creating your company.

Another caveat that should be considered when getting your business going is to be judicious in what you take on. If you sell a product, look at the quality. People will always remember the first pair of shoes they buy from a new manufacturer. If that pair is high quality, comfy, and doesn't cause callouses, they'll buy more. All you'd need to do is concentrate on repeating that process to build a reputation and client base. Don't add a third pair until you have simplified that system.

Anyone will tell you to create a solid business plan first, or at least have an outline. In that plan, make sure you include milestones to meet. It could be something like, by this date, I will do X. A solid plan can take a long time to write—maybe as long as a year or two. Most wannabe entrepreneurs eat a lot of ramen noodles the first year until the ideas and timeline gel. You've never heard of anyone going from pee-wee football directly to the NFL. It's the same with business.

The first year you're excited, but the workload can soon become drudgery. Worry over finances, questioning the idea itself, and waning motivation can make quitting seem attractive. So, my suggestion is to not overdo the development stage. At some point, you have to pull the trigger. But overplanning isn't good.

Stop comparing yourself to YouTube influencers who yammer on about subscriptions or trainings or quick fixes. They're building a following. There are better ways to enter the business world. Start by thinking creatively about setting up your business and how you can save money doing so. Maybe your kids can create a website, or your spouse can edit your videos to post to that website if you ask nicely. I know I just said not to over plan. But you do need a base of knowledge. Take your time, investigate the systems, and don't overcomplicate. Stick-to-it-iveness will make it happen.

Everyone will tell you that owning a company is stressful. You're still doing payroll and emails long after the employees have gone home to a hot meal and their favorite ballgame on TV. Not everyone is cut out for that. Figure out your threshold for pain and misery. There's no shame in feeling miserable. We all go through it. Don't be afraid to call it quits. Adding to that despair is watching a lot of money fly out the door the first year. Have financial reserves set aside or plan to keep your day job to smooth over those first rough patches while you cobble your plan together.

However, you might have a different question. What if my business has plateaued and I don't know where to go from here?

If your business has plateaued, it could be that you're not surrounding yourself with the right people. If you think you're the smartest person in the room, you need to go into another room. Surround yourself with experts in fields you know nothing about.

One of my main messages is to not fall prey to distracting opportunities. It even has a name: Shiny Object Syndrome (SOS). It's a disease of distraction. Entrepreneurs crave new development and technology and aren't afraid to take chances. The danger often lies in their zeal to chase after the newest business opportunity without completing the previous one. They never see meaningful results on the first project. Look at how people jumped on the cryptocurrency fad that has seen a lot of turmoil. Also, early web used CDs that would give you X number of minutes on the dial-up service AOL. What happened? It tanked because technology marches on, often swiftly. It pays to be a slow adapter when it comes to big promises in most fields. As my father used to say, if it sounds too good to be true, it probably is.

Your company culture surely figures into the efficiency factor. Lots of things motivate people—status, benefits, a paycheck, and time off are among them. However, this can be different for each company and person. Many experts have spoken about how to improve your culture. For example, a lot of corporations do team building or networking and family events. Personally, I think these are antiquated ideas. Though they may work for some companies, check attendance at these functions and informally survey employees afterwards. Those statistics may provide insight into whether to continue with them.

I didn't want any more turnover than necessary, as it's expensive and time consuming to find a replacement. So, when I hire people, I want them to buy into the mission of the company and make them feel that they're a part of something more than just a paycheck. I explain the vision and the dream to them and show them how working for me will benefit them—not just the company, but how they can grow as a person. I show them that their participation and diligence will be something that will not only complement the company but themselves as well.

Employees can lose sight of the mission for several reasons. Perhaps they aren't sold on the idea anymore. Sometimes they have personal issues, such as a sick parent or kid, a death in the family, divorce, or loss of income. Life happens. There's not much I can do about that.

Then there are those job seekers who tell you they're interested in your company and its goals. It turns out sometimes they were more interested in getting a job than signing on to my company. It's a perennial issue with hiring: You're always going to run into the problem of finding people who seem like they'd fit, but they don't.

Efficiency can also be eroded by a disillusioned employee. In my experience, there's no way to bring an employee back from disillusionment with their job, the product, or even you as their leader. They'll eventually leave, no matter how much you try to cajole them into staying. I've wasted untold hours trying to change their mind and it has never worked. Their minds are already checked out. Even if they stay, they'll be less productive than they were. If they say they're angry about their pay or vacation policy, that's the tip of the iceberg. It may not even be important what led up to that dissatisfaction. My advice is to get rid of them.

Obviously, you don't want someone around who's not pulling their weight and lets others pick up their slack. That is surely a drag on productivity and makes others resentful. One last piece of advice I have is to be mindful that there's a comfort factor in hiring family members. But I advise against this as well. They know only the same things you do, and it makes firing them a sticky wicket.

—— Summary

In this chapter, I discussed being leery of software or gadgets that promise to solve all your problems. I touched on keeping your policies and procedures clean of any confusing or unnecessary steps. Streamlining them is the way to go. Complicating them frustrates employees and can lead to mistakes. Instead, set your goals and deadlines. Check them daily or at least weekly. Have tools in place to measure and tweak them if necessary.

If you have an online business, a company culture may be a little more difficult to build and foster. Most people like to congregate and feel the busy atmosphere of people working around them. Don't be afraid to let an employee go if they're unhappy. If you don't, that cancer will spread. As a boss, sometimes we become pleasers because we think these employees have something special. If that person has been there two years, they may have maxed out their usefulness. You need to make sure that everyone is on the same page. Don't go the 1099 or temp route, as those people rarely make diligent employees after you hire them permanently.

—— Advice

Take a look at your company. Where do I want to go with my idea? Map it out and

don't compare yourself to others. You started this business because you saw an unfilled niche in the market. So, by definition, you are unique. Obviously, you won't be Coca Cola or Ford Motor Company overnight. Stay real. For example, you could say, "By the time I'm 55, I want to sell this many pool cues, and this is what I must do to accomplish that."

Don't stunt your growth with a lot of unnecessary steps. Trust that your employees are smart enough to fill in the blanks of a not-so-detailed plan. Don't allow yourself to fall victim to items or processes that can hold you back. Keep your company simple, especially in the beginning. It will grow from there.

If you're the smartest person in the room, find people smarter than you.

"Rent a Drunk" companies that provide temporary workers sound like a good idea at first. But these kinds of people are not loyal to your company. Get your own staff instead.

No one will be as dedicated as you are. You can't subcontract your success.

You need to measure yourself on what you do. If you do drop shipping, maybe you can handle it yourself in the beginning. If you run a company that offers services like Angi (formerly Angie's List), make certain your tech people are monitoring your website, which is your lifeline. If the site goes down because the Wi-Fi or electricity goes out, plan how you'll recover. These policies and procedures should be put in place promptly because every minute your site is down, you're losing customers (and you can forget about any SEO happening).

—— Steps

1. Come up with a business plan. Don't jump into anything too crazy.

2. Put some feelers out there about the viability of your ideas—

I'm talking about real experts, not just family and friends on social media. Contact your local Small Business Administration, for starters.

3. When you're ready, apply for licensing and get incorporated.

4. Don't be afraid to do some of the work yourself in the beginning, and eventually hire someone to do it. That way you'll know what the job entails and can hire more intelligently.

5. Create a culture if your company is big enough. Having employees work from home makes this difficult.

6. If you've fallen short of your established goals and timeline, maybe you have to approach things from a different angle. Review them with your team.

CHAPTER 6

My Origin Story

I did not follow a straight line in my business career. Far from it.

My business philosophy, while deeply rooted in my Gen X values, has been shaped by my many experiences in the business world. Some were good, and some (maybe a lot) were bad. But these have all concocted a unique and powerful brew that has made me a success today. As rocky as that road was, if I had it to do all over again, I wouldn't change a thing. Tough times build character, and, boy, do I have a lot to spare.

I went into the Army after high school in the late '90s. Once I was out, I worked in my father and uncle's construction company. We installed automatic conveyors, packaging systems, piping for water and compressed-air, boiler systems, plastic injection molding system equipment in factories, and so on. It was tough work—my back and knees never stopped hurting. But my dad made a lot of hay during those booming economic times. I pitched in where I could with my welding skills.

Our crew traveled around the country, sometimes putting in 15- or 16-hour days, or working weekends and holidays—even around the clock if there was an urgent need. The people I worked with were older guys who liked to drink and do drugs, along with being inveterate workaholics. I learned that last trait well, but, thankfully, not the alcohol and drugs part.

When other 21-year-olds were out chasing girls and going to college, I was hard at work. Looking back, I see now that I missed out on a lot. But even when I had a week off, I didn't know what to do with myself.

The economic heyday that was keeping us so busy started to fade by the late 1990s. Jobs started going to Mexico and China, but times were still pretty good. I should have been thinking about my exit strategy from that business then.

So, when the 9/11 attacks happened in 2001, the world changed in many ways. For instance, manufacturing companies took a nosedive, accelerating my father's business demise as well. The writing was on the wall for everyone to see. Again, I should have retooled then and rethought my direction. But what did I know about planning? No one had ever taught me how to do that.

Eventually, my father was faced with having to close his business, especially since my uncle had fallen ill with cancer. Not having any path to go in, I decided to start my own construction business. It was all I knew.

Lesson #1: Learn What You Can About Running a Business

Just because you're good at doing something with your hands doesn't mean you're any good at owning a business. Running a company is way, *way* different.

Here's what I did to start. I rented the back part of my dad's office and piggybacked on his client list, cajoling old clients to stay with us and sign-up new ones. This is when I learned the art of cold calling. I hated it then, and I hate it now. Sometimes you don't have a choice. The business was not going to come my way by magic.

The first thing I did was look for my ideal candidate to call—someone who I really wanted to approach on a cold call. If you start calling people who aren't to your liking or who aren't your ideal prospect, you're wasting everyone's time. When I first began making those calls, I would research companies to find the employees I wanted to do business with. Then I found out what they were interested in—football, kids, boating, etc. I would open the conversation by asking them about those interests with the goal of making a friend. Nobody likes to be sold something. But they will buy from you if they like you. It takes time to build a relationship. Sure, there were times I didn't want to call. I would sit around and think about why I should call this person because he yelled at me once before. Then I remember my mantra: hunt, eat, or starve.

Practice makes perfect. You must learn not to be afraid to talk to people. The worst the person can do is hang up or yell at you. The first couple of times are awful. Trust me. Your callouses against rejection get built over time. Things can only get better, so keep at it.

Finally, I hooked a client. We put equipment in a company that packaged Gatorade. It was a big job, over $200K. Buoyed by my initial success, I set out to hire people for that job and all the other work I planned to get. I could be just as good as my dad and uncle, I thought. All my efforts were paying off. I was ecstatic and felt I was on my way up.

Lesson #2: Write a Business Plan

I went headlong into this business venture without anything resembling a plan. I was 26 years old, recently married with a new baby, and had no financial cushion. As the main breadwinner, I felt the pressure anyone in this position would. I was determined to be successful. Was it ever nerve wracking! But I put my head down and vowed I would take this chance.

I was clueless about things like spreadsheets, computers, and taxes, not to mention keeping up with the latest technology for my equipment.

Lesson #3: Vet Your Employees

I didn't vet anybody—not new employees, vendors, or customers.

We were so busy that I hired out of necessity. Even though we wound up getting some good jobs, my vendors weren't paying me. Employees stole equipment and money from me. When you're in that situation of desperation, it's similar to being in the jungle. People feed off you like vultures. But, because I had no plan, I was an easy target. I needed assistance, and fast.

I was running on stress. My father was going through a crazy time in his life, so he wasn't much help. I brought in a few policemen to safeguard the equipment, but they were worse than the employees. They were beat cops and had no experience working with construction crews. They sat around telling police stories all day.

Meanwhile, I kept pushing forward. I was taking loans against my house and sold equipment. Employees would come into my office demanding more money. They were parasites (we'll discuss these problems a little later on).

Lesson #4: Adapt to Changing Times

This one failure hit me hard. It wasn't like this in the '90s. With manufacturing leaving the country, both the clientele and employee pool were shrinking. I didn't bring in proper leadership and had no systems or procedures. We didn't automate; I ran the business like it was 1994, and here it was 2005. We even paid employees the same as in 1994. There was no growth or transition. We were still using paper checks without electronically deposit. Most of our work was in file cabinets. We didn't want to incur the extra expense of the cell phone, so we depended on landlines. Talk about late adapters!

Then I hit bottom. We bought a company car for $3,000 to be used exclusively for sales. Don't drive around in this with your family, I told the salesman. Eventually, he threw a bearing, and the car got trashed. I fired him. However, that didn't solve my problems. *I can't keep doing this, I told myself.*

So, I shut the business down. What followed was a severe depression. I parked myself on the couch and stayed there for almost a year watching mind-numbing TV shows day and night. My apathy caused huge problems in our marriage.

Lesson #5: Know When to Quit

It all came crashing down. Our house had been mortgaged (for a second time), credit cards were maxed out, and my bank account was empty. I was chasing money from customers just to pay my bills that week. I could have pointed my finger at the employees, a bad market, the job itself, or the flagging industry. But what good did that do me? I had no one to blame but myself for the failure.

Lesson #6: Have an Exit Strategy

Having some sort of exit strategy would've helped me move past the depression. Just keep in mind that it's best to devise this exit strategy when you are *not* depressed, and preferably when you're on the upswing.

After about a year of living in a daze, I finally got up the gumption to apply to Merck Pharmaceuticals. They make vaccines to inoculate against diseases like rubella, shingles, and chicken pox. They hired both me and my wife. Finally, we were replenishing our coffers. After some years, it became clear that I didn't want to work for anyone else (I forgot to mention that Generation X is a self-centered generation).

So, that's when I began my safety consulting firm (2009 to 2018), where I taught OSHA safety training. I still made a lot of mistakes and was back to scrimping and saving. The business was failing since the training I was doing for all these kinds of services was going online. I didn't have enough money to adapt.

One day, my brother called. He practices law as a plaintiff's attorney in the insurance industry. He said, "I have a career field that I think you'll do well in." I'd dealt with insurance as a safety consultant, so this field felt somewhat familiar. The problem was that I didn't want to leave my kids. But staying in Bucks County, Pennsylvania, would have meant a string of dead-end jobs and certain poverty for me. I had grown up in a family with a slug-it-out mentality. Now, I wanted something better.

So, I packed my clothes, hopped in my 2013 Toyota Rav4, and drove 15 hours straight to Florida where my brother and mother lived (my grandmother had also lived there until her death shortly before I arrived). It all felt right.

To get licensed, I did some online training, was fingerprinted, and served a six-month apprenticeship with Carlos—a guy from Peru. Carlos didn't teach me much, at least not enough to help me with my first case, which was a humdinger.

In 2018, Hurricane Michael was a very powerful and destructive tropical cyclone that turned into a category 5 hurricane.[42] I was assigned to Florida's panhandle for four months. I'd never seen anything like it. Trees were stacked up on the road 30-feet high. There was an eerie silence. Houses were flattened. Mexico Beach was the scariest because it was classified it as nonentry. I went in anyway to survey the damage. There were no people or cars, just ocean, seals, and wind blowing through the rubble. It was an awakening to the power of mother nature.

I didn't know anything about what I was doing. But that's the way it is when you're green. The amount of knowledge I should have acquired was overwhelming. It ranged from things like which form to fill out, who to interview, how to interview, how to assess damage, and what number to affix to the claim. I was stumbling along in the dark.

The first two years as an insurance adjustor were hell. I taught CPR on the side to make some cash and had saved some from an accident payout. I lived in one of my brother's houses. "Just keep working with clients," he said. "You're gonna do well." *Here's hoping*, I thought.

After a couple years, money started trickling in, and business mushroomed.

During those times, I looked at everything as an annuity. It was a mental state of keep pushing and eventually things will come

---

42 "Hurricane Michael," National Weather Service, accessed February 13, 2023, https://www.weather.gov/tae/HurricaneMichael2018.

to fruition. I always kept it in the back of my mind that if I kept getting new clients I'd bring in more sales, and the result would be more income.

Progress meant I had to be dogged about watching my finances to make sure I had money to solidify the growth. The work was seasonal (hurricane season is from June 1 to November 30). I knew people were going to be working for short stints just to get me from A to B. The tricky part was depending on these temporary personnel while I built the notoriety and reputation with clients and vendors. It was a dicey proposition to hire part-timers who wouldn't necessarily sign on to the ethos of the company, but they were a necessary component of my business at the time, and most were serviceable while they were on board.

Now I'm looking at expanding even beyond the 18 states I have licensure for. I was smart enough to invest in 401(k) plans and soon more money started coming in than I'd ever imagined. Things were looking up!

As a public insurance adjuster, I don't work for the insurance company but rather for the individual. I'm a homeowner's advocate. The insurance companies don't like to pay out for compensation. They like to take rights away from homeowners. If a company doesn't get its way, it could go out of business. I understand that. It's a tricky business to maintain growth and serve policyholders fairly. All I can do as an advocate is educate home, property, and boat owners. I tell them the real story about what's going on. They pay me a certain percentage of the insurance payoff in exchange for hassling with Big Insurance. It's a win-win situation.

Now I am on the lookout for other problems that arise because insurance is a rough and tumble business. Companies keep changing the laws so they don't have to pay out as much. When they try to do away with us public insurance adjusters who advocate for clients like those with flattened homes or flooding up to their roof, they try to get laws passed to change the terms of homeowner's policies. Interestingly, these companies also control the checkbook when it comes time to settle a claim. Sort of looks like they're playing both ends against the middle. It's like the quarterback refereeing the game he's playing in. I just don't like insurance companies. They're sharks. They say they want to change things to help the consumer. That's crap. They want to cover their own asses. The industry is a bunch of crooks.

This job is still a wild ride because my clients have all had an interruption in their lives, some quite traumatic, like a hurricane, tornado, or earthquake. I don't need to point out to any who's had a claim that the insurance business moves as glacial speed. Everyone wants their money yesterday, so I get a lot of phone calls with sobbing clients at the other end who have no place to sleep and lost all their worldly goods. It takes patience and empathy to do this job. But I'm good at it because I know what it's like to lose precious items and people that are dear to me. That painful past helps me relate to them about their own grief.

So, I have finally found my niche.

Even though I'm happy where I am now, I'm taking my own advice and devising my exit strategy as we speak. I've learned that lesson, at least.

More Lessons for You:

1. Have a working knowledge of every part of your business, especially in the beginning. I'm not saying be 100% ready— you can't know everything. Figure out what you don't know. Then hire employees to round out that knowledge.

2. Do this work for yourself. When I tried to start my own construction business, I wasn't doing it for myself, and it showed. At first, I didn't know I could even do something in business to please myself.

3. Adapt to the times. I didn't look into the future when the industry was dying. Taking stock of the business and economic climate is a must.

4. Never hire out of desperation. When you're in that situation, you're going to get the bottom-of-the-barrel employees.

5. Have a sales plan in place before beginning your journey. For instance, I could have subbed myself out as a welder at some point and done quite well while I was building up my construction business. Alternatively, I could have created a referral company, like Angie's List, and made a percentage by placing others in jobs. I didn't think that far ahead.

Gen-Xers are rounding the half century mark. We have only 10, maybe 20 years until retirement. Then what? Will everything be hunky-dory when we retire at 65? What about at 70 or 80? Now is the time to ask, "What is my exit plan from the workforce?"

CHAPTER 7

Mistakes

Gen Xers have needed to be more independent than our parents—and more enterprising, too.

But stepping out on your own comes with lots of risks, uncertainty, and mistakes.

A lot of quotes reframe mistakes as a "learning experience" or "dry-run" for success. Those ideas are a cold comfort when you're crying in your beer and have no idea what to do because your business failed, or you've had a personal setback. I like a more hopeful quote that was published in 1832 in New Sporting Magazine: "He who never makes an effort, never risks a failure, and, 'In great attempts 'tis glorious to fail!'"[43]

Those words make me feel like getting up and taking another swing at things, which is exactly what I've done throughout my life. This chapter is about some of my most egregious mistakes either because I haven't kept up with the times or because my early lessons as a Gen Xer have had (and still have) quite a hold on me.

Mouthing Off

In an earlier chapter, I wrote about a woman I offended, quite by accident, by asking if her first name was the same as Stormy Daniels, the adult film star. I was trying to relate to her in a way that turned out to be tactless from her point of view. She told her boss. The boss called me, and did I ever get a lashing. While I did not think I had done anything wrong at first, I now know I made a mistake of likening this woman to someone she didn't find flattering. The same goes for telling someone they remind you of a not-so-attractive person. After all, you wouldn't want someone saying to you, "Hey, you look just like Dracula!" I still think this woman was too sensitive, but I have definitely tailored my approach when meeting women, or anyone for that matter. When in doubt, zip it. This is my motto and lesson learned from that experience. Below are a few others you should keep in mind.

→ **Lesson 1**: I didn't speak up when I realized people weren't seeing me in a way I thought was correct. Stick up for your-self—firmly, but without any energy behind it. I've discovered

---

43 The New sporting magazine. United Kingdom, 1832.

that people's perception of you is rarely what you think you're projecting. And vice versa.

→ **Lesson 2**: When dealing with difficult people, don't be judgmental. Take addicts, for example. Belittling them and trying to get them to abstain from drugs or alcohol is not going to win the day. People don't want to be addicts; they just don't know how to fix it. It all depends on the person. Everyone has demons and you're going to lose people in your life if you become judgmental.

→ **Lesson 3**: Pick your battles. When I encounter unpleasant people, I weigh whether they are worth the fight. It's important not to make assumptions about *why* they are angry. So, when someone gets visibly upset, you can either take it with a grain of salt, or you can argue with them. Just remember to keep lesson 1 in mind. How you see them is not the way they see themselves. Don't overthink what people are thinking.

Please, Please Like Me

I have also mentioned that I was trying to be something I wasn't when I went into the Army to impress my dad. But his view of the military was quite different from mine. He has suffered mightily from his time in the Marines. He didn't choose to go to Vietnam but still answered the call of duty. While there, he was shot in the face, and since his return, he has lived with devastating effects of Agent Orange.

When I enlisted, my dad tried every which way to divert me

from that goal. At the recruiting station where we newbies were collected before leaving for boot camp, he said, "There's still time to get out of this. You don't have to go." But the need to earn his admiration was strong, perhaps too strong, to really understand what he was saying.

Soon, I was in basic training with a bunch of guys from all over the place. That's when reality hit. We all thought, "What the hell am I doing here?"

As a result, I ended up hating the military.

It wasn't until much later in life that I met a lot of vets who served in Vietnam. They told stories about endless body bags, witnessing unit buddies being blown up, shooting little kids, seeing the graves of high school friends and flags in the cemetery—a lot of things that made them cry themselves to sleep. I had not understood the realities of war and its aftermath, such as how your health can deteriorate because of the chemicals used in jungle warfare, ceaseless nightmares because of PTSD, and worst of all, a thankless nation that spat on returning soldiers.

It makes me sick now when I look at these old vets who fought in Vietnam, Laos, and Cambodia. They were young once, maybe even idealistic like I was. I can relate to them better now. All that has helped me finally understand what my father was trying to tell me at the recruiting station. But, back then, I so desperately wanted his respect and admiration. Those needs crowded out my common sense and his wise words. Don't try to be something you're not.

Hi Ho, Hi Ho, it's Off to Work We Gen Xers Go

I must have taken the seven dwarves literally as a kid and developed a work addiction. So many other Gen Xers have the same obsession. I admit, I'm a workaholic. I know there are AA meetings for our kind, but I would never want to stop working to attend one. It's a recipe for disaster.

In my frenzy to make money, I inadvertently ignored the very people I loved so much. I think of all the Christmases, birthday parties, Thanksgiving feasts, weekend trips, ballet recitals, and softball games I missed while slogging away during my 80-hour weeks. This problem began early when I worked for my dad after I separated from the Army. I didn't date, saw very few friends outside of work, and generally lost myself in the job. That's us—burying our head in work so we can keep our minds off the negatives in life.

The problem is that it works too well and exacts a high cost. You never get those moments back, and I did it all because I wanted to prove that one person wrong who'd called me lazy. What I wouldn't do to have one last birthday with my grandfather, or one final recital with my daughter.

Those countless hours also erode your judgment. Do you really think you won't make clerical errors if you work 80 hours a week? Or mistreat your co-owners because you're so crabby? Won't miss out on your kids' precious childhood moments? It's pretty painful in hindsight.

So, find your level of success, but don't forget to come up and for air. It's a huge mistake letting that addiction get the better of you.

Holding on Past an Employee's Expiration Date

This is the story of the costliest mistake of my life that I paid for dearly during the 10 to 12 years of my life that followed. It's my costliest and most important lesson.

Early on in my new public insurance adjustor business, a guy I knew named John gave me a lot of insurance claims. I was glad to have the business because it led to a boom in my portfolio. I was thrilled to be so busy. The problem was I got so busy that I took my eye off the ball in terms of vetting new employees. Things were so chaotic that I practically snatched people off the street to fill positions.

Along came another contractor who said his nephew was getting his insurance license. "If you hire him," he said, "I'll refer more work to you." Obviously, my eyes were too big for my stomach, and I made plans to forge ahead on his generous offer. I agreed to train this guy's nephew as my apprentice for the required six months, just as I had done. I was glad to have the help.

This apprentice kept twisting my arm to change the contract in order to double his commission percentage amount. "I need to make more money!" he kept on nagging me. It would have hurt my business to do that, but we would have been less productive if I'd fired him. Employees were in short supply, so I consented.

As if that wasn't bad enough, he didn't produce much business.

Still, I kept giving him referrals. Unbeknownst to me, he stayed on his six-month apprenticeship license for a year. That meant my name was going on every document and thereby making *me* responsible for the claims. Then, he put the arm on me for an even larger percentage, contrary to what our original contract said.

Along the way, this apprentice brought in his stepfather, Joe. I was told Joe was "well connected in the community" and would bring us sales leads. In hindsight, I knew something was off about this guy. I just didn't know what at the time. Alarms bells should have been going off all over the place, but again, I was happy to have extra hands on deck.

After two years with my company, the apprentice called me and reported that his application for an insurance adjuster's license in Texas was rejected. I asked why. He explained that the authorities found he had a criminal record from brandishing a firearm while intoxicated.

"I lied on my state application," he said. Interestingly, in Texas, you can have a criminal record—you just have to assert it on the application. That issue was never revealed when I hired him or put in terms of my own failing. I never properly vetted him.

Then, the roof came down on my head. After a period of two months, I received a letter indicating that I owed commission payments to the apprentice for 215 insurance settlements that he claimed to have worked on. Determined to get to the bottom of this matter, I called a contract attorney for advice. The attorney informed me that I was indeed required to pay the apprentice. This was a frustrating realization for me.

However, the situation would only get worse. I soon learned that the apprentice had been manipulating the system. He had gone into the company's database and changed the representations of other adjusters, making himself the sole representing adjuster. This newfound information added a whole new layer of complexity to the already complicated situation.

In the year after he left, I had paid him over a quarter of a million dollars. In the meantime, he was violating his contract by calling my clients in violation of his noncompete clause, which he said was not valid. When I contacted his legal counsel stating he was acting in violation of his noncompete clause, their response was, "The noncompete clause holds no validity in Florida."

The contract attorney said their scheme was the classic sucker game that's played out often in Florida. He'd seen it multiple times. Many folks from another part of the country, especially us good ol' Yanks, come down to Florida to set up a business. Meanwhile, the crooks are sharpening their shears ready to fleece us transplants. Their strategy is to bring in their family to take over the business and loot all the owner's funds. Then they sue you to get more. We never did get any business from the uncle after I hired his nephew to be my apprentice.

Upon further investigation of the county records, I discovered this apprentice (along with his friend, the estimator) had four pages documenting a slew of lawsuits consisting of either suing or being sued—not to mention they'd defaulted on several credit card loans. They would apply for a card, max it out to the limit, and then default on the payments. It won't surprise you to learn that they hadn't paid child support either. Very, very bad people. Shame on me for not exercising due diligence.

The lesson here is never trust, and vet like crazy.

People Pleasers

In business and in life, I've found it's a huge mistake to be a people pleaser. This trait has been one of my biggest failings. Most Gen Xers are no stranger to this personality trait. Because we didn't have parental figures at home, we learned to be people pleasers to peers, parents, and teachers to get whatever we needed to get by. We figured that if people liked us, we would get further ahead in all aspects of life. I didn't want to get beat up as a kid, so I was a pleaser. I've carried that trait with me. It's been a character flaw that has been hard to overcome.

People pleasing is not about compassion. It's nothing like giving blood or donating money, and most of the time you're trying to please people who are unhappy. The problem is, you forget about the people who do like you and are happy. Swindlers and other manipulating personalities can sense this trait in you from the git go, especially those who want to take advantage in some way. They end up sucking the life out of you.

Sometimes both people-pleasing and workaholism pair up to create havoc beyond belief. This is what happened with my marriage. I got married way too young at 23. That was what Gen Xers were supposed to do: get a job, get married, and have kids. So, I did. I loved my wife very much. We soon had two beautiful daughters. As I recounted earlier, my employment struggles didn't help the situation much. And because I was a workaholic, I used that as an excuse to put in brutal hours at my job.

Both my wife and I were working at Merck Pharmaceuticals but not in the same department. One day, I received a phone call at work from a lady claiming to be married to the man my wife was having an affair with. I confronted my wife about this accusation and laid down the law, telling her to stay away from this guy (who also worked there), or I would figure out a way to get him fired. She swore that she had never cheated and that she and this man were just friends.

What did I do? I ignored it. The people pleaser in me decided it was a mistake. My wife was too virtuous to do that, I thought. Besides, I didn't want to divorce. I felt I could please her into staying with me and stopping the affair.

The sad result is that she continued the affair. But things took an ugly turn.

She responded to my ultimatum by scheming with her lover to get *me* fired by reporting me to human resources about my threat. It worked. I was fired soon thereafter. I should have walked away from the marriage at that point and said, "You're right. This marriage is rotten to the core." But here I was, zonked out on people pleasing. It must have been the endorphins we get from being so noble and kind. Not listening to my gut was a hard lesson to learn. I would have saved myself a lot of grief and anguish if I'd left her when I found that out. The silver lining was that out of that mistake came my two daughters. Not much else.

Although she seemed sincere in her denial of the affair, a part of me remained suspicious. By 2010, we were divorced. I was still in love with her, even though she made me feel like I was lazy and mean. I took on so much blame that I let her keep the house. Meanwhile, I was homeless. She had cleaned out our 401k and paid all the outstanding bills. I also found out she had secret bank account with her mom.

I let everyone beat me up, including my own family. "You're bad. You treated her horribly," they said. When this all came out about her affair, my dad and mom apologized. "We thought all these years you were the reason for the breakup."

It felt good to have their understanding, finally. But I still blamed myself for that mistake. Call it naivete with a dollop of denial. Still not able to face the reality of my problems, I got therapy. Growing up, we were always told that people who went to a psychiatrist were mentally weak. That was something people told one another to seem better than someone else. This began to change when Gen X became aware of mental health issues. Now visiting a therapist is more widely accepted. I resisted until I thought, *I need this, and I don't care if people judge me. I don't owe anyone an explanation.*

My story isn't unique. Far from it. But what is past is past. Now, let's move on.

CHAPTER 8

Choose Your Heroes Wisely

Good heroes are hard to find.

As part of the MTV generation, I recognized the power of believing in someone or something to give you inspiration and hope.

Religious people believe in their spiritual leader; others believe in a president, their parents, or perhaps a prime minister. A hero is someone who gives you hope, understands of the world around them, and can teach your important lessons. We learn from them and apply it to our lives. A person without hope is easily controlled. As with all people, our heroes may also be flawed characters. But that's okay. It's what makes them real to us.

For example, we have the astronaut John Glenn, President Ronald Reagan, and apartheid activist Nelson Mandela who were tremendously influential when they were alive. When you pick your hero, don't worry what others say about it. Heroes are heroes because they persevere. It's a very personal choice.

I have a few heroes in my life, and most of them are people I've never met. I've chosen them because they resonate with something in my life.

John Quincy Adams

One of my most important heroes and someone I look to for inspiration is John Quincy Adams. In my opinion, he's one of the top 10 presidents in U.S. history. I admire him not because he was president, but because his story is one of honor and duty—no matter what the consequences were of his actions.

John Quincy Adams was the son of a famous president, John Adams, who was a revolutionary and one of America's founding fathers. I understand what it's like to grow up in the shadow of a prominent father. I wasn't named after my father, but John Quincy Adams always had to distinguish himself by using his middle name. I grew up with a dad who was a decorated hero; he even has a monument dedicated to him. I'm so proud that people can look him up in a history book and read about his contributions.

John Quincy was a member the generation that followed his father's. Many of his father's contemporaries were also revolutionaries. We Gen Xers stood in line after the Greatest Generation and baby boomers—people who won WWII and beat the Communists. Now we are coming onto the stage. Like John Quincy, we had a lot to live up to. We keenly feel the pressure.

I admire John Quincy's career after he was president. Most American presidents leave office and don't do anything of importance. He still served the country that his father helped found.

This event, in particular, is the reason I find him so admirable. In 1839, the slave schooner La Amistad forcibly brought captives from West Africa to sell in the New World. These captives rebelled against their abductors even while on the ship and killed the captain and the cook. Once on land, they were granted a hearing before the Supreme Court to decide who owned the slaves. In 1841 at the age of 72, John Quincy Adams, an attorney and member of the U.S. House of Representative from Massachusetts, argued for the Africans. He was roundly criticized for taking their side. But as a staunch abolitionist, it was the least he could do to live up to his principles. He had to deal with this important issue that his forefathers had shoved off onto the next generation, which included his father.[44]

The slaves were finally freed, because as John Quincy had reasoned, they were illegally brought here and were citizens of another country. It's true that he may have ultimately been a failure as a president, and this kind of rebellion against the previous generation is very much a Gen X thing. John Quincy was brought up in

---

44 "John Quincy Adams and the Amistad Event, "National Park Service, July 31, 2017, https://www.nps.gov/people/john-quincy-adams-and-the-amistad-event.htm.

the shadow of greatness and with standards those people wanted to bestow on their offspring. But like Gen Xers, he didn't bend to popular will. He, and many others, resisted those generational constraints and made the world a better place.

This court battle was just one small incident that fell in favor of the slaves. Unfortunately, John Quincy knew this battle was not over and feared the rift in public opinion would result in a civil war. It began a mere 15 years after his death, killing 600,000 Americans who fought over this same issue.

He stood up against adversity, and that inspires me. Don't bend to social norms.

John Clem

Another hero of mine is John Clem. He's a little-known figure of the Civil War. John Clem was nine years old when he ran away to join the Union Army. He became the mascot of his regiment in Ohio because he was too young to be legally inducted into the military and get paid. Instead, the soldiers pooled their money to give him a meagre salary. They made him a little uniform, and he busied himself by running around the camp doing odd jobs. He was a drummer boy at the Battle of Shiloh. An artillery shell hit his drum, so they nicknamed him Johnny Shiloh.

About a year or two later, he was in the Battle of Chickamauga in Tennessee. A confederate officer told him to surrender. John Clem picked up a musket and shot him. For that brave act, General Thomas promoted him to sergeant when he was around 10 years old. He stayed in the Army and fought in a few battles.

At the end of the Civil War, the Army was downsizing. There was really no place for him to go. He was still a kid, but he couldn't go back to school because he had already missed too much. He tried and failed to get into West Point. President Ulysses S. Grant remembered him and promoted him to lieutenant in the U.S. Army. He stayed in the Army until 1915 and was one of the longest serving soldiers. He died with the rank of major general.

Today, we live in a world where people, especially younger ones, are limited in doing things that might not be considered age appropriate. They're either too young to understand or not mature enough to make the right decision about, say, smoking and drinking. But for John Clem, serving his country by being in the military was his niche. That's what I admire—someone who bucks the rules and does what feels right. If a nine-year-old kid can become a major general, there's a lesson for all of us.

My Grandmother, Eleanor

My grandmother Eleanor was a remarkable woman who adapted to life after many of life's sufferings that would have knocked most down for the count. She got pregnant at 19 with my mother. My grandfather married her in 1954. He traveled a lot for work, so, she had to be both mother and father to her seven children in the '60s, '70s, and '80s. She could change a tire, cook dynamite meals, and raised seven kids. I didn't know anyone who could change a diaper faster than she did. She did all that while holding down her union job at a Ford auto plant making brake systems. When she was done working that job, she'd waitress at night making ice cream sundaes. She'd work as much overtime as possible. It makes me dizzy to think about it.

In 1979, my grandmother was following a car being driven by her son Michael (my uncle), which carried her 14-year-old daughter (my aunt). When Michael hit a patch of ice, my aunt flew out, hit her head on a telephone pole, and died. My grandmother witnessed everything. My grandparents never got over that. My uncle Michael was also very distraught that his sister had died when he was driving the car. To numb the pain, he got into drugs and became depressed.

Eight years later, in 1987, my grandfather was told by police that Michael had been murdered by someone. He'd been murdered brutally—set on fire while he was tied up in a car. They never found out who had carried out this act or why. A few years later, I heard from people that the perpetrator was never arrested and got away with his crime.

By now, my grandparents had lost two children in freakishly different ways. Then, in 1989, my grandparents' other son Bill was on a night shift at two a.m. when a drunken driver killed him. He was only 27 years old.

They buried three children in 10 years. No one would blame her for getting depressed and moving a lot slower. In 1996 her brother died, and her husband passed away from cancer in 1999. They'd been married 45 years. That made for four deaths in 30 years.

You'd think that a woman that's had had much trauma would

have sunk into oblivion. But my Grandma Eleanor was special. She was remarried to a WWII fighter pilot who had attended the prestigious Wharton Business School at University of Pennsylvania and knew such luminaries as Lee Iacocca—famed for creating the Ford Mustang and reviving the Chrysler Corporation. She and Jack moved to Florida. "I want to leave you some money," she said to us grandkids, but we told her to go traveling instead. She never gave up hope. We could have been in jail for murder, and she never would have given up on us. It's a loyalty thing.

In the last conversation I had with her before she died, I was stressed out about my own kids because of the divorce and having to leave them behind in Pennsylvania. "Don't worry, Sean. Everything has a way of working itself out."

This woman had two husbands, multiple losses in her life, raised seven children, and never made more than $40K in her life. And she was telling *me* that things will work themselves out!

Here's the takeaway I have from that one small comment she made to me. Anxiety is fear of the future while depression is fear of the past. No matter how bad things get, at the end of the day, we're all going to die. What's gonna happen is gonna happen. You can't control any of it. You can try to direct the future and put things in place, but there's an ultimate plan. All that is a very comforting message for me.

Steve Kitchen

Steve Kitchen was my mentor. He was a generation older than I was. He was blind in one eye but learned how to work with wood from his father, who made hardwood floors. He had several careers and met my father after serving in the Marines.

Steve was one of dad's first employees in his construction business. We weren't close, but I learned a lot about life and business from him.

When I got out of the Army and started with my father's company, the first person I worked with was Kitchen. He knew millwrighting up and down, inside and out. A millwright installs, dismantles, maintains, repairs, reassembles, and moves machinery in factories, power plants, and construction sites. He was a wizard with a wrench. We traveled around installing conveyors and equipment for almost two years. I'd often go on vacations and hang out with his sons, and he was best man at my wedding.

Steve didn't set out to teach me anything, but just watching him taught me the value of hard work and perseverance. His father died when he was with my dad on a job. I'd never seen a grown man break down in tears, and the experience taught me that it was okay to cry.

The one special gift he gave me was teaching me how to fix things with my hands. I can figure most things out today because he taught me how to use my mind *and* my hands. So, I learned how to fix things when I didn't have the proper tools and became ambidextrous in using any device if crunched spaces didn't allow me to use my dominant hand.

Another lesson I learned from Kitchen is that there's nothing wrong with this kind of work, and that I should take great satisfaction in building things and watching your work grow in front of you. He respected his trade, and so did I. There's great honor and dignity in blue-collar work.

He passed away in 2012 of leukemia. He had worked at Three Mile Island during the partial meltdown of one of the reactors in 1979, and it was believed that his exposure to working there led to his illness. Toward the end of his life, he regretted that he'd missed so much because of the astronomical number of hours he worked each week.

I relish having been exposed to those kinds of skills. There was a time when vocations like welding, masonry, and plumbing were trained by men who had to do it for a living. They passed it down to those of us who would listen. Unfortunately, there are a lot of Gen Xers who don't know how to work with their hands.

I think of Steve Kitchen every time my mom asks me to do something around the house. We need collectively to teach those skills to people.

—— Summary

You need to have people you aspire to be like, no matter how flawed they may be. It's valuing the goodness and spark in them, along with what they provide and teach you in their path in life. Their lessons can teach you lessons that you can use as a salve against the bumps and bruises you will get as from your own trials and tribulations.

—— Advice

Pick your own heroes. It doesn't matter what people have to say about them. Strive for greatness just as your heroes did. Remember, to err is human, but your heroes can give you a helping hand.

CHAPTER 9

Reading the Room

Poker players know a lot about body language. Identifying someone's "tell" is their stock-in-trade. A tell is a player's behavior or demeanor that gives away information about the strength of their hand. Those clues can be as subtle as raising an eyebrow. It may also be unconscious or deliberately misleading. But those tells can also include hints you might never notice, such as a cracking voice, twitchy fingers, or even gulping or swallowing. I've even heard that players with a weaker hand will talk or laugh too much, blink excessively, or fidget with their clothing or jewelry. In contrast, pressing one's lips together can signal a strong hand. Look out!

These tells, or micro expressions, may last only a one thirtieth of a second.[45] Jury consultants make megabucks by reading jurors' reactions during a trial. They see things like someone rubbing an arm, head scratching, or squirming, and know how to decipher it. Some signals tell the consultant that the jurors don't like the way the attorney is addressing the witness, for instance. Those 12 jurors can provide a lot of data about how they're receiving the information.

Just as poker players and jury consultants learn to read others' tells, you, too, should be on the alert for any suspicious body language or evasive behavior—whether it's in the workplace, on a date, or at home. When I say be on the alert, I mean checking in with your gut often, because someone's body language that seems a bit off often triggers a sensation in your body. So, it's imperative that you learn these nonverbal cues, but most important, you must trust your hunches. They came from somewhere, and that somewhere is that person sitting across from you.

This is all to say that words are often secondary to what people broadcast with their movements. It's often not just one element but several. Psychologists call these cluster clues, which is a group of movements, postures, and actions that emphasize a common point. If you try to interpret body language from a single gesture, it's like trying to find the meaning of a book in a single word. Individual elements of their tell may not be obvious. Instead, I've learned to key in on a person's overall attitude. That is far more revealing than any single sign. So, identifying the meaning of those

45 David Matsumoto and Hyi Sung Hwang, "Reading Facial Expressions of Emotion," American Psychological Association, May 2011, https://www.apa.org/science/about/psa/2011/05/facial-expressions.

clusters provides a more accurate picture of what is being "said."

This chapter is about all the tells that I have encountered when it comes to judging the sincerity and truthfulness of people's words and actions. My term for this is *situational awareness*, which goes beyond whether a client is tapping their fingers or exhibiting shifty eyes in a business meeting. Call it my cynical Gen X approach to life.

My mantra has always been to read the crowd. As humans, we usually ignore danger around us. We don't normally fear that someone is building a bomb or that lightning could split our house in two. It would overload our senses. But we are animals after all. A rabbit wouldn't live very long if it didn't heed the signs of a hawk circling above. Reading your situation can help you avoid some uncomfortable situations in the business world, and, I might add, the dating scene too. Once you know what to look for, it can save you time, money, and emotional strain.

The trick is to train yourself so you can recognize these signals. Oh, sure, anyone can see a person is holding something back if they bite their lip or frown a lot. The more subtle indicators, like the ones those the newbie poker player gives off, are unconscious.

Some card players are so good at controlling their body language that they can produce what are called false or even reverse tells. These are the Olympians of the cheating world. The secret to their success may lie in the fact that they have convinced even themselves that their lies are true. They can look you right in the eye and fib like all get out. Those people are pathological. It's pretty hard to defend against them. Watch out for these vipers.

The signs can differ depending on who you're reading. Are they subordinates? Clients? Prospects? Investors? Employees? They all have different reasons for meeting with you and expectations of the outcome. But the bottom line is that you have to excite them. People generally dislike meetings and having to listen to someone blather on about this or that product, or how the supply cabinet has been looted. You have to make it worth their while. So, I recommend breaking the tension.

Some of these gurus are consummate showmen and women and come out on stage dancing to music. Others who are psychological and ask a difficult question to start off. They know how to get the crowds attention. Business leaders know how to get people wound up, and you're antennae should go up when you encounter these kinds of people. Remember, nobody does something for free. If they tell you that, then *you're* the product! Take *Facebook* or *You-Tube*. They don't care what you do as long as your eyes are glued to the screen to take in all their delicious ads.

Read your crowd. If you walk into a room and feel people are unhappy or tense, you may need to switch up your presentation. You don't have to acknowledge what you sense in them. You merely address it in a certain way. Perhaps tell a joke or start with a funny story. If you don't, you risk losing them.

If someone is bored or daydreaming at a meeting, you can easily assess that by how their eyes dart around or how they nervously turn away and look towards the door. Of course, this is an obvious tell. But it's a signal that you should quit. Walk away. What if their posture isn't right, like they're slumped in their chair or playing with their phone? One-on-one meetings make it easier to spot these kinds of indicators. I was in a meeting once with a job candidate for a high-level position. When she sat down, she pulled out not one but two phones and set them on the table in front of her. I could hardly believe my eyes. *Am I taking up too much of your time, lady? Expecting a call from the president? Forget this candidate!* I thought. I couldn't get her out of the office fast enough.

The same thing goes if you're being stalked by a salesperson or other individual wanting something from you. Everyone, it seems, is trying to separate you from your money. And the myriad scams out there are like cockroaches. They never go away. They may be updated to conform to, say, a digital world, but they are here to stay. So, if someone is trying to talk you out of money like in a Ponzi scheme or "I'll double your money" kind of thing, don't be afraid to up and leave. That's situational awareness. If someone is trying to get you to change your morals and their posture isn't right, or their attitude comes off in their voice, take flight.

I have a good story about my ex-wife. I didn't know until some months after we were divorced that she had been having an affair (talk about not reading the clues). About six years after it was official, I discovered something as I was waiting to take my daughters for the weekend. I'm a prankster, but I had no idea that this trick of mine would elicit a huge tell from her.

We were sitting on the couch. I took off my sunglasses and looked straight at her. "I know what's been going on," I said. "I know your secret." In reality, I didn't know *anything* about her affair. I was just messing with her. But, boy, she got so nervous that her eyes went up and down and back and forth. She stared at me for a second or two, then looked away. Just from her shifty eyes, I knew something big was up.

By this time, I had lost all feeling for her. Without the need to love and be loved by her any longer, I was able to read her body language and eye roll more easily. Her face told me everything I needed to know.

My suspicion she was hiding something big was confirmed later when she admitted she had been having an affair for most of our marriage and many years beyond. The silver lining in this story is that she thought I knew all about it then, all because of my prankster personality.

Always listen and watch, and you will find out more than you think.

These signals that something is not right may not be strong enough for you to act on them right away. Then, maybe six years later, you find out they were the crook of the century. I'd love to know what signals Bernie Madoff, the guy who swindled his investors out of billions of dollars, was giving off. Nobody was reading his body language, that's for sure.

Ex-FBI Agent Joe Navarro recommends in his book, *What Every Body is Saying*, to look for behavior like someone fiddling with a paper clip, trying to change the subject, or not looking you in the eye.[46] A fishy handshake should warn you not to trust that person. But if the new acquaintance's handshake feels like a vice grip, that

---

46 Joe Navarro and Marvin Karlins, *What Every Body Is Saying: An Ex-FBI Agent's Guide to Speed-Reading People* (New York: William Morrow Paperbacks), 2008.

person may be too controlling. A firm handshake is just right.

Unfortunately, you may not become conscious of these signals until after you have been screwed. Take the time those guys were ripping me off. I wasn't aware of their scheme then. But I knew something was fishy when I asked them a question about missing equipment. They took a second or two to answer. It's not a math question, guys! Where are all my wrenches? What's happening is that they're thinking of a story to tell you. It may have been a split-second pause. But in hindsight, it told me volumes.

I used to be a bouncer in several bars. Wow, was that ever an education in reading people. I like to say that alcohol is the ultimate truth serum and can lower a person's ability to monitor their behavior. It turns them into an open book.

When you work at a bar, you learn that a lot of people are party animals and just want to let off steam. But there are many who frequent the place because they had a lot of pain and suffering. They're depressed or lonely, are in a bad marriage, or had something happen in their life, like a death or illness of someone close. So, they self-medicate with alcohol. People who live in bars have demons, and they try to exorcize them with Johnny Walker or whatever's on tap. Maybe both. Misery loves company.

Then there are the proverbial barflies whose glory days are long gone and they haven't done much since. I became acutely aware of who was an alcoholic. I was always amused by the many ways these poor souls tried to hide their addiction because they were embarrassed by it.

Lots of them have gotten stuck. They've been out of school 30, maybe 40 years and were still stuck in the same routines hanging out with their high school buds. Sometimes underage kids would try to trick me into getting drinks. I eventually left my job as a bouncer because the environment became too much.

You might well ask why I didn't see the signs from these creeps who soaked me for a lot of cash. My excuse is that I was too busy to pay attention to the signals that were blaring at me like a bullhorn. In my marriage, it was a little different. I was blinded by the need to stay married to the woman I loved. I didn't *want* to see the signals.

I've spent a lot of time trying to reconcile that lack of awareness. I booted myself all around the room a thousand times whenever I got duped. But these people who prey on others are experts at lying. That's how they make a living and have been practicing their skill for years—perhaps decades. You come along with your Pollyannish outlook, thinking the best of people, and pow! You get it in the kisser but good. I've met a lot of smart people who should have known about these kinds of swindlers. And they still get snookered.

I have a friend who calls this kind of thing the cost of doing business. It's a kind of schooling that you didn't ask for but got anyway. I am sadder, but oh so much wiser now.

CHAPTER 10

It Ain't Easy Being Green

Gen X's independent, resourceful nature lends itself well to starting a business.

And despite being overshadowed by boomers and millennials, Gen X is leading the way in small businesses. We're good at finding new ways to do things and solving problems ourselves.

There's an adage that says when you start a business, it's like you're married to it. I find this to be so true. Sometimes you reap the rewards, and other times you get stung. Then there's the cranky quote from Steve Jobs. "I hate it when people call themselves 'entrepreneurs' when what they're really trying to do is launch a start-up and then sell of go public, so they can cash in and move on. They're unwilling to do the work it takes to build a real company, which is the hardest work in business."[47]I think Fry's quote a bit harsh. On the other hand, there's no reason to go into this without being fully informed about what lies ahead. Even though when people say, "I'm here to help," is overused nowadays, in this case, it's accurate. My chronological list of items below can help you prepare to launch your dream company.

Once you decide to take the leap, congratulate yourself. You've just taken the most important step. It's a challenging, frustrating at times, but also rewarding—and let's hope—lucrative as well. Of course, every business venture comes with a risk. So, roll up your sleeves and delve into some finer points about starting out not addressed earlier in the book to help you avoid or at least lessen that sting.

Starting out can be nerve wracking. We go into these kinds of endeavors with all the hope in the world. Visions of dollar bills dance in our heads. Too often, though, the missing ingredient is planning. Many eager businesspeople just pick out a name, get business cards, and go off to the races. They *sort of* know what they want to do. They are either ignorant of the steps they need to take or they are not sequenced correctly. That's why they fail. At the very least, that's why *I* failed. I finally wised up when I started this insurance business. While things have generally gone smoothly because I've been down a lot of these roads before, I still have shock waves from the unexpected.

---

47 "Steve Jobs Quote." Lib Quotes. Accessed April 4, 2023. https://libquotes. com/steve-jobs/quote/lbo1m2q.

The bumps along my road have not been because I didn't know what to do to start out. My problems have been due mostly to the crunch in clients needing help when a hurricane or cyclone levels everything in the areas I service. Claims skyrocket and can go unanswered by insurance companies for months, or even years. Meanwhile, my clients are left homeless and dabbing their eyes over irreplaceable possessions, photos, and family heirlooms that are gone forever. Because I had started other businesses, I anticipated most of the problems with this one. That said, no one can know everything, and, as noted, being an entrepreneur can be risky.

Do you want to do a side gig to provide a side income? Just know that it may not scale up for quite a while. It's not a bad way to test the waters, and you can do it on weekends to see if you want to do it full time. Do keep in mind though that it can be exhausting to have a hustle like this on the side and maintain good performance on your regular job.

On the other hand, if you want to commit to starting a business you intend to do 100% of the time, you must be engaged in your business 100% of the time. Here are some steps to help you succeed:

1. Before doing anything else, be crystal clear about what you're going to offer. Are you a B2B or B2C business? Whichever it is, start something that *nobody else is doing*. Come up with a name that tells something about your product or service. Who do you want to sell products to? Or if you're a nonprofit, what population do you want to serve?

2. Research, research, research. The more you do, the more

success you will have. Ask friends and those in your field what you should look out for. Most valuable are those who have nothing to gain from helping. Talk to the people at Small Business Association (SBA) or SCORE (a resource partner of the SBA with volunteer business mentors). They offer webinars, courses, local workshops and roundtables, online resources, and free mentoring.

3.   Know the kind of client you *don't* want to work with. If I frame houses, there's no harm in asking a roofer or concrete person about a particular client. They have nothing to lose because you're not in a related industry.

4.   Rough out your plan in the months before taking incorporation or filing tax forms or marketing. Look at it every day. Critique it. Map out a timeframe (just don't drag it out too long). What are your goals? What is your exit plan? Consider this to be your marriage contract. Make sure you want to commit to all of it. This lack of planning becomes painfully clear when payroll and money issues pop up, as they always do. You can count on that being the case as much as you can count on the sun rising in the east. Think ahead about what you will do when money is in short supply. Will you take out a loan, or borrow from your parents? Do some stocks or bonds you can cash out? I hired a marketing firm to write a business plan, and it was a huge waste of money. It was this cookie-cutter document that was way too generic for what I wanted to create. So, I wrote my own. I've changed it often since starting out. I learned not to rely on anyone else to create my dream company. Save money and do it yourself. Now that's a pretty Gen X trait!

5. Next, incorporate your business in your state unless a legal advisor tells you otherwise. It can be done through an accountant, attorney, or LegalZoom.com. There are many choices: LLC, S Corp, C Corp, or a nonprofit 501c3. Consider all of these options before setting this up. Be sure everything is legal, bonded, and insured. What might be legal in Virginia may not be in North Carolina, so you'll need to familiarize yourself with all city and state laws and ordinances.

6. File your company name. A word of caution: If you're thinking about filing your form from, say, September to December, wait until January (unless it's an emergency) because you'll be paying taxes for a time when you probably won't have any income.

7. Research your audience, which includes your clients age, ethnicity/race (if these are important), buying habits, income, and education. Think of this as anything that may be pertinent to your product and sales pitch. There's no sense in paying for advertising for those who are not likely customers. This may seem obvious, but I receive an untold number of ads through social media, email, and snail mail that have nothing to do with my life. They've wasted their money because they didn't do their homework.

8. Next step is your marketing and sales plan. I'm assuming you budgeted for this. Scope out costs for ads in newspapers, TV, radio, direct mailing, online (and if so, which sites), flyers, and business cards. I used to have a handy metal, electronic business card that could transfer my information

directly onto someone's phone simply by tapping it. It's fast and safe, but you must be in person to do that. So, it is also an inefficient way to spread the word about your company. It is way cool though. I know people give out business cards like candy at Halloween, but how many cards do you have lying around so you can call that guy you met at the bowling alley who does driveway paving? Besides, most people look for contacts online now.

9. Determine how often you will advertise and monitor its efficacy. (I wrote earlier about SEO companies. Please be careful about hiring one of them.)

10. Determine your goals for revenue and how you will get there. Perhaps a one-, five-, or 10-year plan would help you achieve those goals more readily (and rejigger if necessary after your first milestone).

11. After all that's been put together, find out from someone in your state's licensing bureau about cost and turnaround time for your application. Whether it's roofers, hair salons, or fish mongers, they all need licensing.

12. Go to the bank to set up a business account. Determine whether you pay employees by check, ACH, PayPal, or another option. Put your business name on the check and not your personal one.

13. Once you've finished with the bank, talk to a CPA or attorney about legal ramifications. Make sure he or she specializes in the field—so, not a divorce attorney. Do they have an idea of what you want to do and what the legal ramifi-

cations are?

14.   Get marketing material together including finding a solid
      web designer. In the beginning, you only need a landing
      page that you can add to later.

Now comes the hard part.

In the beginning, you may have to do any or all the following
yourself: sales, marketing, physical work (such as setting up your
brick-and-mortar store, handling stock, etc.), business development, closing deals, and bank transactions.

By now, you have your business plan, your company is incorporated, you've filed tax forms, spoken with an attorney about any
liability, and gotten licensed with the state. It may also be good to
price similar goods or services around your area. This will help determine whether your charges are greater or less than the standard
rate. Too cheap and people think you're not good enough; too expensive and clients may think you're gouging them. Here's another
short list of other things you'll want to consider:

1.   Whoever your clients are, you must get in front of them. No
      hiding behind a social media site! Once you've figured out
      who they are, hammer that message home again and again.
      Don't be surprised if it takes six to eight months before you
      get your first client. Take it from me, you will bend over
      backwards to please them.

2.   Dress the part and be sure to always look professional.
      When I was growing up, the teachers all dressed profes-
      sionally. Women teachers wore a skirt or dress. Men wore

ties. The only person who didn't was the gym teacher who wore shorts, a T-shirt, and a whistle around his neck. I called teachers sir or missus and I still do. None of this first-name stuff like today. Gen X still has that respect for authority. It seems that we've lost that now. I see men wearing sweatpants when they teach, and there's no divide between leisure and school. In short, if you want to do business with CEOs, you must dress like a CEO.

3. If times get too tough, seek out a spiritual leader, life coach, or therapist to talk to. I did and it saved my bacon. I felt so good to vent to someone who didn't have a horse in the race. Spouses don't usually cut it since they will tell you want you want to hear, not what you need to hear. Life coaching is very important. A mentor can guide you through your problems. You're going to be stressed and angry a lot of the time, but if you can vent for a little bit it will keep you sane.

4. Last, and this is very important, pay yourself first or you're never going to have anything left over. If you pay everyone else first, you'll lose interest in the whole venture. Meanwhile, everyone else has made money off you, and you have empty pockets.

—— Advice to Self

I'm in my middle years now and I'm beginning to take stock of where I've come from and where I'm going. So, what advice would I give my younger and older self? Here is what I decided.

I have only two people to answer to: my eight- and 80-year-old self.

When you are eight years old and in the third grade, you think high school seniors look like old men and women. You have very little memory of people until you're about that age. Soon, you begin to evaluate people and situations. I would ask my eight-year-old self to look at me at my current age and ask, "Are you impressed that I've become a father and had a successful business?"

Now, when you're 80 and sitting in a rocking chair on a porch in your twilight years, you'll more than likely be conducting an inventory of your life. I will ask this old man, "Did you make it all count? Are you a burden to your family? Did your moral and religious and business successes count? Did you provide for your loved ones like you promised?"

Everyone dies. Only memories and your name on the headstone survive. In 100 years, not much will matter about your life except whether you took care of your family. They will remember because, even though they may not recall specifics, subsequent generations will remember or at least be affected by your efforts to protect them—just as the knowledge that your forebears taught you has been passed down to others. You honor their memory by carrying out that same responsibility until you are 80 years old.

Did you find love? make friends? get to do all the things you wanted to do?

There's still time to do all that and more. But starting your own business? Fantastic.

A famous Gen X song, "Everybody's Free to Wear Sunscreen," was a classic when it came out in 1999. It sums up our Generation X philosophy and rhymes with the message in this book. Do what's important now before it's too late, like getting to know your parents, not being too hard on yourself, or worrying about the future. Forget the trivial and focus on what's important. The lyrics are part nostalgia, part advice that that's often easily forgotten—like staying close to your siblings because friends come and go. Remember the compliments you receive, not the insults. The only hard and fast rule is to wear sunscreen.

Being an entrepreneur is as exhilarating as it is exasperating. But the "Sunscreen Song" tells us to not sweat the small stuff. When you are 80, you can look back and see you carved a path no one else has. You're an original! You may not have planted a flag on Mount Everest, but the journey you will set course for will be just as noteworthy and well worth the effort. It is your gift to the world.

Now, what are you waiting for? Let's get to work!

Acknowledgments

I would like to express my deepest gratitude to all those who have helped me in writing this book. First and foremost, I would like to thank my friends Matt Moore and Steve Shelly. Matt, a simple house painter with a love for history, has been a constant source of support and inspiration throughout my life. His unwavering belief in the power of learning and the lessons of the past have been a guiding light for me.

Steve, my attorney and friend, has been a mentor to me for many years. His wise counsel and his deep understanding of the law have been invaluable to me, both personally and professionally. He has taught me that the law is not just about rules and regulations, but about taking care of people and doing what is right.

I would like to extend my heartfelt gratitude to my siblings Joyce, Sheila, and Aaron. We grew up in a split house, and although we faced some challenges, we managed to overcome them and make our way in the world. Sheila's courageous battle with cancer was truly inspiring, and Aaron's achievement of an advanced degree and his career in law has been an inspiration to us all. Joyce has shown us the true meaning of love through her long and loving marriage to Kevin, and her unwavering support for her family.

I would also like to express my appreciation to my nieces and nephews, the children of Joyce, Sheila, and Aaron. They have grown into remarkable individuals who have taken risks and worked hard to make their parents and their Uncle Sean proud every single day. Their determination and achievements are a testament to the values instilled in them by their parents and our shared upbringing.

I would like to express my deepest gratitude to Chief Warrant Officer Shawn Woodhams, a man who has dedicated his life to the protection of his country and family. As a veteran of multiple wars, having served in both the United States Marine Corp and United States Army, he embodies the true spirit of what it means to be an American patriot. With a rifle in one hand and a Bible in the other, he is the closest thing to a modern-day Minuteman that I know. After growing up on the wrong side of the tracks and leaving for basic training a week after graduating high school, Shawn never let his past or anyone hold him back. He has shown us all what it means to be a true American, father, husband, and a man of honor. His unwavering commitment to his country and his family is an inspiration to me.

I would like to express my deepest gratitude to my grandmother, Louis Mathis Kling, and my step-grandfather, Fred Mathis, for their unwavering love, support, and guidance throughout my life. My grandmother worked tirelessly throughout her life, holding down multiple jobs while still managing to raise her children, and then babysitting multiple grandchildren, great-grandchildren, and even great-great-grandchildren well into her mid-80s. She was the premier cook of macaroni and cheese and a quiet and patient woman who never left the side of any of her children, not even when they lay in hospice care. Fred's love for the outdoors and hunting showed me the beauty of nature and how to experience the world as God painted it. He was an exceptional Jeopardy player, hardly ever missing a question, and showed me that knowledge is something to be pursued and cherished.

I would like to express my deepest gratitude to my grandparents, Charles "Harry" Battis and Eleanor Battis, for their unwavering love and support throughout my life. Harry's love for animals and working with his hands showed me the importance of finding pleasure in the simple things in life. His dedication and hard work to protect his family were evident in everything he did. He is sorely missed by all those he touched in life. My grandmother, Eleanor, was a fighter and a hardworking woman who dedicated her life to her children and grandchildren. Together, the two of them helped shape me into the man I am today. My love of all things history comes from them, and their unwavering support and guidance have helped me achieve my dreams.

My father, David Kling, I want to take a moment to express my deepest gratitude and appreciation for all that you have done for me throughout my life. You have been a constant source of love and support, always there to lift me up when I was down, and to share in my joys and triumphs. Your life story is truly remarkable, and I am in awe of all that you have accomplished. From serving in the Marine Corps and being a Tunnel Rat in Vietnam, to starting a successful business and coaching youth sports, you have lived a life full of adventure, courage, and selflessness. Your dedication to helping others has been an inspiration to me and everyone who knows you. Your generosity, kindness, and compassion have touched countless lives, and your commitment to making a difference in the world is truly remarkable. I am honored to be your son, and I am grateful for the many sacrifices you have made on my behalf. You have always been there for me, no matter what, and I cannot thank you enough for your unwavering love and support. Thank you for being an amazing father, role model, and friend. I love you more than words can express.

My mother, Debbie Kling, I want to take a moment to express my deepest gratitude and appreciation for all that you have done for me and for others throughout your life. You have been a shining example of selflessness, compassion, and kindness, always putting the needs of others before your own. Your dedication to caring for the elderly as a medical assistant for 25 years is a testament to your generous spirit and your unwavering commitment to helping those in need. Your presence in the room when both of my daughters were born is a memory that I will cherish forever, and I am grateful that you were there to share in those special moments. Your love of bowling is a testament to your unwavering spirit and your zest for life. Your dedication to the sport for almost 60 years is a true testament to your tenacity and your love of competition. But above all, it is your love for your fellow man that truly sets you apart. You have spent your life in service to others, caring for the weaker and the less fortunate, and your kindness and compassion have touched countless lives. I am honored to be your child, and

I am grateful for the many sacrifices you have made on my behalf. You have always been there for me, no matter what, and I cannot thank you enough for your unwavering love and support.

My beautiful daughters, Katherine and Virginia, I want to take a moment to express my deepest love and gratitude for the joy and happiness that you have brought into my life. You are my greatest creations, my masterpieces, and I am in awe of the strong, smart, and kind women that you have become. From the moment you were born, you showed me what it truly means to love someone with all your heart. Your first steps, your birthdays, your graduations, and all of your wins and losses have been a source of pride and joy for me, and I am honored to be your father. As you continue to grow and pursue your dreams, I know that you will conquer the world and make a difference in the lives of others. Your strength, intelligence, and kindness are an inspiration to me and everyone who knows you. I only held your hand for what seemed like a moment in time, but you will hold my heart forever. I am grateful for every moment that we have shared together, and I am proud to be your father. My only hope is that one day I make you as proud of me as I am of you. You are the light of my life, and I am grateful for every moment that we have shared together.

To the many inspirational people in my life, I am humbled and grateful to be surrounded by so many amazing individuals who have touched my life in countless ways. Each of you has inspired me to reach for the stars and to never give up on my dreams, and I am forever grateful for your dedication and support. Ed Bell, Sgt. Kyle Minorics, Warrant Officer Jamie Viars, Kyle Mayhew, Duncan Reed, Jerry Rogers, Dan Geiger, Bryan Weidemoyer, Jared and Greg Gaingiulio, Tony Maggio, Harry Lippincott, Pop Dietze, Uncle Eddie, Aunt Jeanie, Jessica Battis, Jeremy Bishop, Jack Christwell and so many others, you have all been a source of inspiration, strength, and encouragement for me. You have given your time, your talents, and your energy to help me achieve my goals, and I cannot thank you enough. Your unwavering dedication to my success has been nothing short of amazing, and I am so grateful for the positive impact you have had on my life. You have challenged me, motivated me, and helped me to become the best version of myself, and I am forever indebted to you for your kindness and generosity. To each and every one of you, thank you from the bottom of my heart for all that you have done for me. Your support and encouragement have meant the world to me, and I am so honored to have you in my life.

With deepest gratitude,

Sean Kling